PROLEGOMENA TO A CRITICAL GRAMMAR

VIENNA CIRCLE COLLECTION

Editorial Committee

HENK L. MULDER, *University of Amsterdam, Amsterdam, The Netherlands*

ROBERT S. COHEN, *Boston University, Boston, Mass., U.S.A.*

BRIAN MCGUINNESS, *The Queen's College, Oxford, England*

VOLUME 2

EDITOR: BRIAN MCGUINNESS

JOSEF SCHÄCHTER

PROLEGOMENA
TO A CRITICAL GRAMMAR

Foreword by

J. F. STAAL

University of California

D. REIDEL PUBLISHING COMPANY
DORDRECHT-HOLLAND / BOSTON-U.S.A.

PROLEGOMENA ZU EINER KRITISCHEN GRAMMATIK
First published by Julius Springer, Vienna, 1935
This edition translated from the German by Paul Foulkes

Library of Congress Catalog Card Number 72–77879

ISBN 90 277 0301 9

Published by D. Reidel Publishing Company
P.O. Box 17, Dordrecht, Holland

Sold and distributed in the U.S.A., Canada, and Mexico
by D. Reidel Publishing Company, Inc.,
306 Dartmouth Street, Boston,
Mass. 02116, U.S.A.

CONTENTS

PART ONE

THE NATURE OF LOGIC

PART TWO

ON THE GRAMMAR OF WORDS, SENTENCES,
AND COMBINATIONS OF SENTENCES

FOREWORD TO THE ENGLISH EDITION

POSITIVISM, and with it the Logical Positivism of the *Wiener Kreis*, is nowadays increasingly disliked. There are good and bad reasons for this lack of popularity. One of the objections is that, like its close relatives, behaviourism and operationalism, positivism as a philosophy seems to ignore the meanings of sentences and more generally the intentions and feelings of people. This has led some to brand it as an instrument of reaction paving the way for the manipulation and exploitation of human beings and their aspirations. Yet the Vienna Circle itself aimed at the destruction of the then current traditional metaphysics, which was rightly considered (as emphasized by Otto Neurath) the vehicle of social and political reaction: it sought to destroy it precisely by offering logical positivism in its stead. Much in these criticisms is anyway due to academic, not to world politics. Even today positivistic trends continue to loom large in the Establishment of academic philosophy (and certainly that of the social sciences, which lag behind even the development of philosophy). But at the time of the Vienna Circle the Establishment of academic philosophy was almost entirely made up of metaphysics, and only positivism managed to defeat it – at least temporarily, and in the English speaking countries.

Many philosophers, even those who dissociate themselves from metaphysics, claim that they deal with conceptual analysis of some kind or other and are therefore not accountable to empirical test. Though positivists also developed the view of philosophy as a non-empirical discipline, they did not adopt so squeamish an attitude, but aligned themselves more closely with the dirty work of the sciences. It is not surprising, then, that the most striking – and, it would seem, the only decisive – refutation of positivistic tenets in the philosophical realm has come from outside philosophy, viz., from the study of language, especially from the development in linguistics called generative transformational grammar. Linguists have shown that it is impossible to account for natural languages in an adequate manner if these are conceived only in terms of speech behaviour, observed utterances or sequences of sound, as would seem to be required by a positivist methodology. But when human language cannot be accounted for in positivistic terms, neither can man himself. Now, this refutation affects only classical positivism directly, and is not as clearly applicable to the logical positivism of the Vienna Circle. But the distinction between classical and logical positivism had not always been appreciated by philosophers, and least of all by linguists or linguistically-oriented theorists of language. There are various reasons for the resulting confusion. To linguists it seemed that Bloomfield, the main proponent of American structural linguistics and as such one of the targets of Chomsky's attacks, aligned himself with logical positivism by publishing, in 1939, a volume entitled 'Linguistic Aspects of Science' in the *International Encyclopedia of Unified Science*, a classical manifesto of logical positivism, edited by Carnap, Neurath, and others of its proponents. What was widely regarded as the typically positivist emphasis on observables was rampant among the structural linguists, who tried to erect, e.g., syntax on the foundation of 'observable morphemes' (culminating in Harris' *From Morpheme to Utterance* (1946)). When the transformationalists showed that unobservables (e.g., rules and structures on which rules operate) have to be postulated, it was clear that they went not merely beyond structural linguistics, but also beyond classical positivism. But many linguists and not a few philosophers went further, and to them logical positivism seemed to be refuted as well.

Yet the differences between classical positivism and logical positivism are profound. Logical positivism has been mainly responsible for the trend to go beyond phenomenalism and to accomodate theories and theoretical inferences. It is true that semantics was originally neglected in the logical positivist camp. For Schlick, the meaning of a sentence was contained within its verification. For Neurath, to pass from language to meanings was to reintroduce the transcendental entities of metaphysics. But Schlick came to believe, like Wittgenstein, that questions of meaning, unlike questions of fact, are solved by indicating the rules of the logical grammar which we make use of in order to describe reality. Carnap developed, partly under Tarski's influence, theories of meaning and paid a great deal of attention to questions of meaning and to theory formation. It is true that widespread *lectophobia* or fear of meaning, which pervades much of contemporary philosophy (witness Quine) and is not absent from contemporary linguistics (where even most generative semanticists give credence to syntactic arguments only), can be traced back to classical and early logical positivist prejudices. (The 'verifiability theory of meaning' itself is an attempt to exorcize the object of such fear, for meaning and sound are equally basic and mysterious – it is only their complicated relationships through language that are now receiving a little light.) However, the logical positivists increasingly stressed the *logical* character of the positivism involved.

The failure to distinguish clearly between classical and logical positivism and the resulting belief that they shared the same weaknesses might not be so widespread if more had been known about logical positivist views regarding natural language. That relatively little attention has been paid to this is partly because it was not clear where one should look. Schächter's *Prolegomena zu einer kritischen Grammatik*, rare even in libraries and here for the first time offered in English translation, enables us to re-evaluate the position of logical positivism with regard to language, to retrace some of its alleged weaknesses and to discover its widely ignored points of strength. One of the interesting conclusions that emerge from its study is that this logical positivist's analysis of natural language is much more profound than the allegedly positivist, structural linguist's analysis would lead us to expect. This is not so apparent from the few more well-known works dealing with language in the tradition of logical positivism. The best known of these are Carnap's *Logische Syntax der Sprache* (1934), and its successors such as *Meaning and Necessity* (1947). Also Reichenbach's *Elements of Symbolic Logic* (1947) might seem to belong here (not the work of Wittgenstein, who was a philosopher or metaphysician, and at no time a theorist of language). But Carnap dealt almost exclusively with constructed languages and the chapter of the *Logical Syntax* dealing with 'General Syntax' is not quite as general as its title indicates. Reichenbach's *Elements*, on the other hand, contains a long chapter entitled 'Analysis of Conversational Language', which provides many insights that can be properly described as belonging to the semantics of natural language (Reichenbach, moreover, quoted not only from English, but occasionally also from Turkish). Schächter's work appeared in 1935, and so could not make use of Carnap's *Logische Syntax*. Neither Carnap in his later work, nor Reichenbach, seem to quote Schächter's book, which therefore stands in splendid isolation as the best specimen of the logical positivist analysis of natural language.

The object language to which Schächter applies his analysis is German. His translator into English, Dr. Paul Foulkes, has not only provided a reliable and readable translation, but has also substituted appropriate English examples for the German examples of the original – a procedure that of course is not trivial, but has necessitated constructions of considerable novelty.

Relatively little space of Schächter's book is devoted to a logical positivist theory of language. Much attention is given to the logical analysis of a variety of linguistic relationships. Much of this is clearly incompatible with a classical positivist methodology. Many of these logical investigations are not surface-oriented but betray a keen sense of underlying semantic relationships. It is instructive to witness how an avowedly positivist philosopher discovers facts of language which so-called positivistically-oriented linguists – albeit obsessed by almost mythological matters of procedure and methodology – had not been able to detect. More recently linguists and logicians, unhampered by positivist dogma and methodological paranoia, have been able to go further.

Schächter is keenly aware of the distinction between some of his analyses and those of the grammarians of his time. He blames them, for example, for constantly being in search of the subject of a sentence, which leads them to call the 'it' of 'it rains' a subject. "Grammarians here need to ponder their actions" (Part Two, II, 6:9). Elsewhere he explicitly formulates the distinction between the grammarian's task ("the grammar of material") and his own ("the grammar of meaning"), illustrating this distinction with a reference to chess (an illustration that had been used by both de Saussure and Wittgenstein): "The grammar of material may be compared with a book on chess that is unlike the usual ones in concentrating more on the externals of the game, such as the appearance of the pieces and their consequent classification, with only occasional hints on moves and positions. What would correspond to the grammar of meaning is a treatise on chess dealing mainly with moves and positions while material is discussed only to the extent that it is relevant to them" (Part One, III, 1:2).

The most interesting observations and suggestions in Schächter's book are those that relate to the logical analysis of natural language. Why then, if these are so interesting, has this work been so much neglected? I believe that the causes of its neglect are largely historical and, when thus considered, fairly obvious. While Schächter's *Prolegomena* deals with many different features of natural language, logicians in general had been content to study, analyze and idealize only certain artificially isolated fragments of language – e.g., those involving logical connectives and quantifiers. By the time logic became less restricted, took inspiration once more from Aristotle, and began to consider, e.g., modalities and tenses, Schächter had been forgotten. In the wake of the recent slow convergence between logic and linguistics, many more features of natural languages are beginning to receive logical attention. The belated English edition of Schächter's *Prolegomena* therefore occurs at the right time.

Berkeley, October, 1971   J. F. STAAL

TRANSLATOR'S FOREWORD

This book is the first English version of *Prolegomena zu einer kritischen Grammatik*, published by Julius Springer, Vienna, 1935, as Volume 10 of the Vienna Circle's series *Schriften zur wissenschaftlichen Weltauffassung*. The prefatory remarks of both editor and author acknowledge the influence of Wittgenstein in a general way. However, in aim and approach, the work differs from Wittgenstein's *Philosophische Grammatik* (1969). This is indeed based on material going back to 1932, some of which Schächter must have known. On the other hand, the present Prolegomena not only explains the general, philosophical principles to be followed, but in the light of these proceeds to cover the entire range of conventional grammar, showing where that is uncritical. Whether Wittgenstein in his turn knew of Schächter's work has never been explored.

Schächter's object is universal grammar. As is natural, the examples in the original are largely drawn from German grammar, with occasional minor excursions into other languages.

For English readers, what matters are the general problems of grammar: there is no point in tying these to the linguistic peculiarities of German, let alone a local variety of it. One who can grasp German at that level might as well read the original.

The translation is therefore twofold: the text as a whole has been rendered into English, and the entire apparatus of examples has been replaced, as far as this can be done, by illustrations from English grammar, chosen so as to bring out the same kinds of problem as in the original.

In some cases, no serious difficulties arise, since English and German are indeed fairly closely related within the Indo-European family of languages. Nevertheless, they are different enough to prevent the choice of appropriate examples from being entirely a matter of routine. For in their ambiguities, whether syntactic, semantic or functional, the two languages are far from parallel.

Insofar as the examples differ, the present version is thus not in the narrow sense an exact copy of the original. Since new examples had to be chosen in any case, their content has, where necessary, been adapted to matters more likely to be familiar to the English reader.

Finally, as to technical terms: according to context certain terms in the original have to be variously rendered in translation. Indeed, in a few places the original is itself ambiguous. Of these problems, one in particular requires special mention: the terms 'Sinn' and 'Bedeutung'. Much confusion about these stems from Frege's paper *Über Sinn und Bedeutung* (1892), in which he gives the latter term a special technical meaning, namely whatever it is that a sign refers to. The new term is introduced in the most offhand manner without any explanation, almost as an afterthought and without any attempt at underlining the radical departure from established usage. Frege, having stated that we must distinguish that to which a sign refers, simply adds that we may call this its 'Bedeutung'. The coinage is as unfelicitous as it is pointless, since German already has a word for what Frege wants: 'Bezugsgegenstand'. Albeit not too elegant, the term is clear and not eccentric. The mistake about 'Bedeutung' springs from a misreading of idiom: the verb 'deuten' with the preposition 'auf' and the accusative, means to point to something, whence a confusion with the verb 'bedeuten' could tempt one to the Fregean move. It is the sort of punning on vocabulary that Hegel used to practise, except that he had a better understanding of language.

It has been argued that Wittgenstein adopted the Fregean notion of 'Bedeutung', but the evidence for it is unconvincing. For example, the 1922 translation of the *Tractatus Logico-Philosophicus* renders 'Bedeutung' as *meaning* in 3.33; and *things (his signs) mean* (i.e. Fregean 'reference') in 3.331. Such a violent shift in usage from one paragraph to the next cannot be imputed to Wittgenstein. Indeed, it is quite unnecessary in the context, and is not required, as some suppose, to make sense of Wittgenstein's discussion of Russell's Theory of Types. Thus D. F. Pears and B. F. McGuinness are right in their translation (4th impression, 1969) to render the term as *meaning* in both cases. Schächter uses 'Bedeutung' in its ordinary 'sense', namely that of *meaning*, what one looks up in a dictionary. 'Bedeutung' is what words have. 'Sinn', on the other hand, is what sentences have, namely *sense* or *significance*. A word may have various *meanings* and may be used in various *senses*. A sentence may have *sense*, and it may *mean* something (in the sense of having a certain function), but it does not have *a meaning*. What complicates the case even further is that the ordinary German word for 'significance' in the sense of 'importance' is 'Bedeutung'. Some linguistic charting is called for here, but that, in the main, is a German worry.

Meanwhile, we follow Schächter and render these terms in the spirit of his original and in the 'sense' that English idiom requires.

As to the philosophic presuppositions behind Schächter's enterprise, detailed discussion belongs elsewhere. The task of the 'Prolegomena' is achieved in that they do make out a case for critical grammar.

February, 1971   PAUL FOULKES

EDITOR'S INTRODUCTION
TO THE GERMAN EDITION

This volume of *Schriften zur wissenschaftlichen Weltauffassung* (Essays on the scientific world view) differs from previous ones in style and intention, in that it is propaedeutic in character. It aims to introduce and prepare: prepare for a serious study of logic and grammar, and introduce a genuinely philosophic treatment of them.

The books ordinarily used for teaching these subjects are philosophically most inadequate; above all they fail to satisfy those who have won through to the conviction that genuine philosophic problems are in the end grammatico-logical in the deep sense in which 'critique of language' coincides with 'critique of knowledge'. The author of this book received his philosophic training under the influence of this conviction (first stated explicitly by Ludwig Wittgenstein) and he could thus set himself the task of presenting to a large circle of unprejudiced readers who seek enlightenment these first steps required to attain a grasp of logical and grammatical questions, without getting lost from the start in the lush psychologistic and metaphysical thickets that have been let grow up round them over the years. I think Dr. Schächter has resolved his task well: his account is plain and simple, his exposition fresh and without learned cant. In some places I disagree with the author's views, but this concerns special questions the answer to which are not essential to the basic attitude. That a book has been accepted into this series is not to say that the editors share all the views expressed in it, but merely that they think it has value and serves the end to which the collection is dedicated.

If widely and carefully read, this book can, I think, be most useful, for I am convinced that it is effectively suited to direct the reader's attention towards an understanding of the 'grammatical' by producing in him the genuine philosophic attitude. That the book does not mention philosophy itself and that many propositions in it seem at first trivial, is in accordance with our method of philosophizing, which likes to begin with the elucidation of the seemingly evident and unproblematic, wishing to excite a sense of philosophic wonder before the problems become hopelessly tangled in the struggle of dogmatic opinions. Anyone teaching languages or philosophy at introductory level, should regard it as quite essential to gain a clear view of how grammatico-logical questions arise. To teachers of these subjects especially I should like to recommend this book; I am convinced that it could exercise a very favourable influence on teaching in secondary schools. Besides, reading it may give hints and insights to anyone who on his own pursues philology and logic.

Vienna, June, 1935   M. SCHLICK

AUTHOR'S PREFACE

This book aims to present an easy to grasp account of my views on the foundation of a critical grammar. The task of critical grammar is a logical completion and improvement of traditional grammar. Wherever conventional theory of language has failed to read off correctly from usage the rules current in language, critical grammar is to fill the gap.

In this book, as in an extensive account of critical grammar on which I am currently working, my aim is to keep the account in the kind of philosophic spirit for which, I believe, the enquiries of Ludwig Wittgenstein are the model.

Many sections of this book resemble warning notices and road signs that are easily overlooked. The reader might therefore always observe what prejudice is being guarded against in any section or what logical reflection might thereby be suggested.

I thank all those who have most kindly helped with the manuscript and its publication, especially Prof. Moritz Schlick, and Mr. Friedrich Waismann who have constantly advised and assisted me and Dr. Hans Nowotny who has given much useful help in the preparation of Part I.

Vienna, June, 1935   DR. JOSEF SCHÄCHTER

PART ONE

THE NATURE OF LOGIC

CONTENTS OF PART ONE

In the following chapters, on language, the language of science, the relation of logic to grammar and psychology, we shall use examples to illustrate what logic itself is. Only after struggling towards a correct view of the nature of logic can one pursue grammar in the critical way.

CHAPTER I

SIGNS AND LANGUAGE

(1) German, French, English, Latin, etc. are languages. Here we wish to talk about *language*, and to begin with we mean one of these languages, all of which seem to us equivalent in this context; that is, the facts we must examine are almost the same in all these languages, so that it is indifferent which of them we select.

(2) However there are language types, whose structure differs greatly from ours. These we shall not examine here, at most we shall occasionally use them as auxiliary models to clarify the structure of *our* language. We shall even *invent* linguistic models for this purpose.

(3) We know that language may be used for various purposes. One may use it to describe experiences, to express feelings, give orders, request, ask and so on. However, all these functions presuppose that there is a means for *expressing* something: on this they all depend. We call it a *sign*. To 'express' a word here means not only to speak or write: in the sense here used even any unspoken thought expresses something.

1. USE AND MEANING OF SIGNS

(1) Anything we call a sign is *used* in a certain way. We say that a sign *means* something.

(2) When we speak of the use of an object, we mean that we employ it in our actions as a means to some end. Similarly with the use of signs: they are means for certain actions. We employ them to give orders, utter wishes, curse, quarrel, reconcile ourselves, pursue philosophy and so on.

(3) What distinguishes signs from one another? We say, their meaning. To see what this meaning is, let us first observe how one imparts a meaning to somebody who does not know it. This happens in several ways: (i) As with children, by pointing to an object or performing an action, while pronouncing the word. This results in the child using this word whenever such objects or actions supervene. (ii) By means of sentences. This happens for instance in the teaching of a foreign language, which

itself serves as the teaching medium. The sign (or word, since words are signs; see 5) is here clarified by its *context*, that is by those sentences in which it occurs. (iii) However, we can explain a word also by adducing sentences in which usage *does,* and others in which it *does not,* allow its occurrence. These are the *rules* of use. We sometimes speak of *use* for short, intending the necessary and sufficient rules. The meaning then consists of the various kinds of use, that is of the rules that hold.

In the phrase *rules that 'hold',* the 'holding' refers to *linguistic usage,* which we come to know by observing how members of a language area use the signs, by asking people in what sentences the signs may occur, and so on.

(4) Knowing the meaning we can use the sign. By stating its use we exhaust the meaning of the sign. Thus a person knows the meaning of a sign, when he knows how to operate with it and how to place it in its linguistic context.

2. Laying down conventions of use

(1) We distinguish two features of signs: (i) What is used for the purpose of denoting, which we may call the *material* of the sign, things like lines of ink on paper or chalk on blackboards, sound waves in speech and the like. Here, too, belong presentations or other mental processes that go with thinking, though this insight presupposes rather more lengthy reflection. (ii) Laying down a convention about the material so that it will be used in a certain way (the rule of use).

(2) The word 'sign' has various meanings in language. Often it means material as above, wherever we contrast a 'mere sign' with its meaning. However, we will not call mere material a sign, since it is the laying down that the material shall be used in a certain way that makes it a sign in the first place. The convention chosen and the material together constitute the sign, not the material alone.

(3) This is often overlooked. We are so used to regard for instance red lines on trees as way-marks, that we are not conscious that they are not just red lines that by themselves mean way-marks, but that it is the convention chosen that makes the lines into signs. This becomes clear when we observe how a scholar and a savage respectively look at a document.

3. 'ARBITRARY' CONVENTION

(1) The laying down of the mode of use or meaning of a sign is arbitrary: we can lay down about any material how it should be used. The following examples are to show what we are to understand by 'arbitrary' here.

(2) The ancient Greeks at first thought that the words of their language were linked with things and belonged to them like properties. This prejudice is easily removed by pointing to the existence of other languages.

(3) With this prejudice removed, a more complex one threatens to arise. It is well known that there are onomatopoeic words, for example to knock, to prattle and so on. One knows how they are connected with accoustic phenomena. What has caused selection of these sounds is here obvious. With other words it is more difficult, but there, too, there must be causes which it is the task of linguistic research to discover. Besides, a word may change and develop both in its material (sound shifts) and in its meaning (semantic shifts). This tempts one to regard the conditions that have led to a given choice of material on the one hand and to changes in material and meaning on the other as the *function* of the sign. Our insight that none of this has to do with the function of signs may be put by saying that the function of a sign is laid down *arbitrarily*. (We use the word 'arbitrary' here to separate what *caused* the usage of a sign from its *ground*. See Part Two, III, 4).

(4) A 'tacit convention' (to be discussed in 5 below) may likewise be described as 'arbitrary'. For although we use a sign without conscious decision of will, anyone speaking a language can always reject one sign and decide for another. In this sence the choice of a certain mode of dress or of a certain kind of utensil may be described as arbitrary even for somebody who knows none other nor reflects on other possibilities. For although he accepts the given mode as a matter of course, he could choose another were he to ponder the question. The word 'arbitrary' simply means this possibility and not any actual decision of the will.

4. SYMBOL – SYMPTOM, TWO ASPECTS

(1) The words 'sign' and 'meaning' are used in another sense as well. When for example we say that the barometer's falling is a *sign* of imminent rain, or *means* the approach of bad weather, we use them in a sense

different from the previous one. The difference may be indicated by the words 'symbol' and 'symptom'.

(2) To counteract a stubborn confusion of symbol with symptom, let us consider some examples. Suppose in a geography lesson a pupil is asked the number of inhabitants of London and he gives the correct answer. We may examine this in the two ways mentioned: (i) The spoken sentence "London at present has so and so many inhabitants" tells us something about London. In that respect the words are signs and the sentence a combination of signs. (ii) We can interpret what the pupil has said as a *symptom*, for instance as showing that he has acquired the relevant facts. Here then we have one utterance that is viewed in two ways, somewhat as we might view a coin: either as to its value, its position within the currency system, or as to shape, which reveals something about production methods at the mint.

(3) Further, consider the following situation from fiction: a tramp bound for a village uses the sign language of tramps to leave behind a sign that means 'there is a police station in the village'. A second tramp who passes by and understands the sign will take good care not to enter the village. For him the sign is in the first place a *symbol*. He does indeed infer that another tramp must have been here but his attention is directed mainly to the sign's meaning, namely 'there is a police station in the village'. A policeman who is out to detect tramps when suddenly confronted with this sign from the language of tramps will infer that a tramp must have come this way, he treats it mainly as a *symptom*. The meaning of the sign does not greatly interest him. We may compare this with the attitude of the recipient of a letter who happens to be a graphologist.

5. WORDS AS SIGNS

(1) The spoken language of words has sounds as its ultimate elements. These sounds as such, that is without a convention, have *no* meaning. However, this ability to produce various sounds has been utilized to link meanings with them. Therefore the spoken words of language are signs.

(2) Here we may distinguish between two possible kinds of convention. Either the way a sign is used may have been preceded by an explicit convention, such that one says: sign X is to mean this or that – is to be used thus or thus; or a sign may be used *as if* it had been laid down. The

latter is meant when we speak of a 'tacit convention'. The two conventions are here equivalent, as may be clearly seen from the following common example: a child often has a nickname besides its true name. This last was specifically laid down for the child, chosen by the parents and legalized by the authorities by entry on the birth certificate or baptismal register, a use explicitly laid down. The nickname on the other hand may have arisen in various ways and then established itself. Once it has done so it will be used and understood and, being used frequently, may well displace the proper name. This establishing itself of a nickname has certainly a cause, as in the parallel case of a custom or usage – it is not our task to enquire why. What is important for us is that the nickname *does the same job* as the specifically laid down proper name. Since the two names do not differ as to *use* but only as to origin, in logic we can ignore this difference. The material of a sign, and the way it is laid down, are alike, indifferent to its function.

(3) Up till now we have considered spoken language. Since one cannot always communicate through speech, one 'makes use of' another human ability, namely that of distinguishing different marks made for instance on paper, laying down that certain sounds be *correlated* with certain marks. This is a system of signs whose material satisfies the requirement of permanence and thus can convey something to many for a long period. Written language consists of signs as does speech, except that the rules of use concern different *material*. This confirms our earlier point that in laying down a sign we may choose the material at will.

As to sounds and marks, we may safely speak of *correlation*, while avoiding the term as easily tending to mislead when relating signs to 'things'. An example will make this clearer: if I have ten apples and ten pears, I can correlate them (to ascertain that they are equally many without counting them in the ordinary way): I pair them off, or I make a mental note (big pear left – big apple right and so on) where the characteristics used may be immediately forgotten so long as I know that certain items have already been correlated. Correlation is a way of looking at things that presupposes that things have some name or other. When I put a pear alongside an apple to correlate them, this means in words that for any further operations this pear and this apple are to count as a correlated pair. But 'this pear' and 'this apple' are signs (proper names, see Part Two, II, 1). Likewise in making mental notes, 'the big pear left' is a name.

Not so in 'correlating' signs with things, where the latter have *by definition* no name. But one cannot correlate linguistically anything that has no name. The word 'correlation' can here mean only the substitution of a certain symbol for another less serviceable one such as: this thing here.

6. WORD AND SENTENCE (SIGN AND EXPRESSION)

(1) So far we have spoken mainly of signs while nevertheless using the word 'sentence' without close examination. Let us now see what lies at the basis of the distinction word – sentence (sign–expression).

(2) By expression we understand any utterance, thought, wish, request, memory and so on within any language, what is denoted as a sentence in the widest sense and that with which we operate once the signs have been laid down.

(3) The distinction sign (word), expression (sentence) and combination of sentences is a matter of grammar: for the sake of an over-view of language one constructs schemata where in the first case one leaves aside sentences and in the second combinations of sentences. Leaving aside sentences and looking only at the 'dictionary' of the language, one obtains the signs.

(4) The difference between word and sentence can be variously shown: by pointing to negation, truth and falsity, probability and so on. A sentence can be negated, it can be true or false or probable, it can be fulfilled, obeyed, answered; none of which holds of the isolated sign, the word in the dictionary.

(5) When I explain to somebody the meanings of the words 'book', 'table' and so on through pictures by showing him various photographs of books, tables and so on, he will be able to understand these words without yet using them in a sentence. We say: his language consists of single unconnected words. Usually, however, he combines words into units that serve not only to *name* things, but also to *report* about events and so on. We then say: his language consists of sentences.

(6) A sentence cannot consist of one *single* sign. This seems paradoxical. The objection is that we know monosyllabic words that constitute commands for example; this is accompanied by referring to the appropriate linguistic facts. However, such objections are based on a confusion of 'material' and 'sign'. For if the monosyllable expresses a command,

its material is simple but the meaning is articulated in so far as according to the structure of our language the sign is to be translated into a sentence (unless that structure admits no such analysis). This translation thus shows that there are at least *two* concepts that are united into a sentence.

(7) The elucidations here sketched are methods to bring out as clearly as possible this difference – familiar to all of us – between word and sentence (see Part Two, I, 10).

7. LANGUAGE AND SYSTEM OF SIGNS

(1) We can compare various languages, or various stages of a single linguistic evolution and thus distinguish between more and less developed languages. The difference can be shown in two ways: (i) In terms of the vocabulary, that is the number of words, so that the greater number is the criterion for belonging to a higher stage. (ii) In terms of the possibility of forming sentences with the given words. On this criterion a tribal language consisting of 100 words and capable of fewer sentences would be less developed than one having fewer words but allowing more sentences to be formed. Of two languages capable of the same number of sentences, the one that allows a further combination of *sentences* (as for instance by means of the words 'and' and 'or') would have to be taken as the more developed.

(2) Additions to the vocabulary in the sense of the first criterion may be compared with the steady advance of the series of natural numbers, while additions in the sense of the second criterion corresponds to the introduction of the various operations, such as multiplication, permutation and so on.

(3) The distinction between systems of signs and language can be drawn by applying the second criterion. A system of signs is a language consisting of signs but not admitting operations, as for instance collections of nautical signals and so on. But our language consists not only of single signs and systems of signs, it contains also *operational* symbols which produce various combinations.

(4) We use the concept 'language' where we have not only signs and systems of signs, but where operations occur as well, according to special rules of *combination*. For a system of signs it is enough to have *some* substitution rule. If one have the two signs 'water' and 'stone' without

using either for the other, we may speak of a *regulated* system; but language contains systems of signs and operations.

8. The Vagueness of Words in Language

(1) The words of language are often vague and usage fluctuating.

(2) For example our language contains the words 'book' and 'booklet'. There are cases in which anyone using them can justify himself in terms of linguistic usage. A book of 500 pages will never be called a booklet (except in jest, when it really means a big book); on the other hand a small book of a dozen pages or so will readily be called a booklet. Between these two we can imagine a series of intermediate cases in which on various grounds one might object to one or other of the words.

(3) In this connection we distinguish three areas of use: to the first belong all those cases where usage *admits* a sign; to the second, all those where it *excludes* a sign; and to the third, all those where it allows no decision. (For a given material will be used to designate other things so long as they retain some similarity to the original object so designated, until it is *gradually* put out of use through loss of similarity.)

(4) Suppose someone ask us: can we say that animals trained to approach on hearing a certain sign of a bell *obey* this sign? Here we must note the following: (i) When applying this word to man, the question simply does not arise, usage is unambiguous. (ii) For objects like table and chair and so on nobody (except animists) will speak of obeying. In between we have the reactions of animals and plants, which more or less resemble either man or object. To the above question we would reply: we are free to call this behaviour 'obeying' or not. (Poets extend the first area at the expense of the second, the sleeping apple, the laughing sun, the merry wind and so on, see Part Two I, 13.)

(5) Usage in turn depends on actual fact within a spatio-temporal region. A European who travels to central Africa visiting the pygmies and then reports on what he observed, might call a table he saw there (assuming they had them) a small table, whereas the pygmy (if his language allows the distinction between table and small table) would call the reporter's small table simply a table, while perhaps describing a big European table as a house without side walls. It is the given circumstances of life that *motivate* specific conventions. (On motivation see Part One, III, 4.)

(6) Another linguistic phenomenon that is sometimes mixed up with vagueness is the following: there are different signs for the same thing – we call such words synonyms – and also the same sign for different things – words with several meanings. An example of synonymity is: rope, cord. An example of multiple meaning is the word 'constitution' (meaning natural condition of body or character, basic guiding principles of government, material make-up of a substance). Synonyms represent a kind of linguistic abundance, multiple meanings an economy. This distinction has nothing to do with the vagueness mentioned earlier, for these words can *furthermore* be vague or not.

(7) It is very important to observe the facts of vagueness and multiplicity. Many misunderstandings that occur in everyday life and in science (differences of view) can be explained by this characteristic of language.

9. THE MEANING OF WORDS IN SCIENCE

(1) Let us now ask: what makes the difference between the meaning of words in everyday life and that in science?

(2) In the language of science it often happens that a word from everyday life is given a meaning quite different from its ordinary one. When in ordinary language we speak of force, this has nothing to do with the force of physics. The choice of identical material was indeed guided by certain similarities, but the rules of use are different. Similarly in many cases where everyday words are used in science, words like inertia, work, colour and so on. When we consider these words in their scientific use we can say that the signs derive their material from ordinary language, but the rules for their use are quite different.

(3) This fact alone does *not* capture the difference between the two languages, since both in everyday language and in physics the same words may be variously used, so that various rules may have been laid down for the same materials. The differing rules of use cannot constitute the difference between the two languages, for we have already observed that within everyday language itself the one material may be variously used (multiplicity of meaning).

(4) One might think that everyday language must be inexact, and so, therefore, must the insights, accounts and so on that are couched in it. This holds only insofar as one gives no precise meaning to the signs

of ordinary language; but once one declares for a fixed meaning, description will no longer be vague. In ordinary language, time indications such as 'until Friday', 'I study only during the day' may be meant as approximate or precise, depending on circumstances. Questions like "is 'until' meant to be inclusive or exclusive?" (or "does the expression 'day' cover the last second of the day?") are asked only where it matters. Indications of time, orders of things and series of events show doubtful intermediate stages and transitions ("is it the last element of the first domain or the first of the second, or both at once?") and it is a matter of sharpening the language to assign the 'doubtful' elements to *one* domain. But where one feels this not so important one refrains from giving further precision (this would be called 'splitting hairs'); in that case a question as to membership of a borderline case is misconceived. For here language has by convention renounced the question; or rather, its concepts are as though defined in a way that precludes such questions from arising: if someone asks them, he must have defined the concepts differently.

(5) Accordingly we can say that everday language is as it were a large reservoir of signs that may be used vaguely or more precisely. The language of science partly coincides with everyday language insofar as the vague meaning *contains* the more precise; but partly not, insofar as the two languages merely share the same material. Thus the word 'until' in its 'vague' meaning contains both the inclusive and exclusive concepts; but the word 'work' has a different meaning in physics.

(6) The difference as regards vagueness may be described as follows: in everyday language a sign has a variable meaning, while in the language of science it has a more precise one, laid down beforehand for scientific purposes. We are using the comparative here, for in science, too, words are not always unambiguous. The difference is one of degree: the point is that in science we try to overcome vagueness.

CHAPTER II

CONCERNING THE FORMAL

(1) To characterize the language of science from a different point of view, let us consider certain circumstances within so-called everyday language. Let us imagine that a man has spent some time in France to learn the language, and on his return we put a French book before him to test his knowledge of French. Suppose this book is written for sailors and concerns the events of life on board ship, using many special terms about manoeuvring with sails and so on; or we may suppose that he is shown a book on the life of workers in a particular firm. Suppose we observed the fact that they were expressions or whole passages that he could not make out. Could we then say that he does not know French? We should have to deny this, for a Frenchman who was not a sailor or a factory hand would be similarly embarrassed. This reflection makes us see that only certain words and their combinations fall under the imprecise description of 'everyday language', and these are common to all special languages of sailors, factory workers, farmers, engineers and so on. For example, the words 'and', 'left', 'table' and so on occur in all these special languages, and likewise words that denote activities that are independent of one's calling, such as 'go', 'eat' and so on. The special languages differ from everyday language in that their concepts are less vague, they exhibit new concepts and leave modified and usually smaller scope for certain words.

(2) The following examples will make clear what we understand by 'scope of a concept'. Someone who has no connection with shipping may well distinguish aquatic vehicles into boat, ship, steamer: these words have wide scope and can denote anything that the expert denotes by brig, barque, schooner on the one hand and by frigate, corvette on the other, as well as yacht, keel and so on. We observe that such terms are formed whenever one examines a certain field more thoroughly (the sea, industry, forestry, mining and so on). Similarly in science: since the sciences treat certain fields in more detail (inorganic, organic, psychological processes and so on) than is done in everyday life, new

terms arose, with new and usually narrower scope (which further made possible the formation of many new and reliable sentences). Through being more intimately occupied with a field one is led to make existing words more precise and to introduce quite new terms that sometimes do and sometimes do not share the material of signs in everyday language.

(3) We may now imagine that language itself becomes an object of such special treatment. Concern with language and its structure can lead to the coining of new terms just as dealing with the above-mentioned fields can.

(4) Let us first clarify by means of some examples what is peculiar to a concern with language. Suppose in a French lesson at high school the verbs in -er are being studied. For the sake of practice, the teacher, having discussed the paradigm 'donner', asks a grammatically well-informed pupil to conjugate the less familiar verb 'envelopper'. The pupil runs through all active and passive forms to the teacher's satisfaction. After school the pupil accompanies the teacher who now uses only French. The pupil wears his coat collar wide open. Since the teacher is concerned about the pupil's health – it is a freezing winter's day– he advises him "enveloppez vous, un peu mieux, mon cher". Curiously enough, the young man does not react as expected. When asked why, we find that he does not know what 'envelopper' means; that is, he does not know how to use the word *outside* grammar. This shows that we can select words from a language in order to study them only from the grammatical point of view: we can deal with them as if they were not otherwise used in language.

(5) Another example: in teaching chess, an instructor can proceed by practising with his pupil the rules of the game, in such a way that in the usual sequence (move – counter move) the pupil moves his pieces according to the prescribed rules. One may ask: are these two playing chess or not? To start with we must say that they do, for all the rules are being obeyed. But in another sense we might say that they do not, for they are playing merely to demonstrate the rules of the game, they are doing its grammar. So long as it is viewed merely as demonstrating rules, it does not yet belong to the game; but as soon as we abandon the way of demonstration, we are playing chess. (To decide whether it is a case of *demonstrating* or actually *using* the rules, one can do no more than ask the players or infer their intentions from their behaviour.)

(6) In our first example, the pupil has mastered part of the demonstration although he cannot yet use the word. For we can distinguish two ways of operating: (i) Operating with signs *within* grammar. We speak of grammar so long as we are concerned with rules and their demonstration. A grammar lesson may even include illustration of the use of the word 'envelopper' and indication of the sentences in which it may occur and in which not. All this forms part of producing the meaning, of the 'prolegomena' for the mode of use. Suppose the teacher now pronounces the above sentence during a lesson, to make clear its use: 'Enveloppez vous'. It is hardly likely that any pupil will start wrapping himself in a scarf. For they all know that it is a case of demonstrating the meaning. (ii) Operating with signs in life and action *by means of language*, that is in the way in which the solicitous teacher in our example used the word 'envelopper'. In what follows we shall distinguish between a use in grammar and a use in applied language.

(7) Before proceeding, consider an example that exhibits the difference in the opposite direction to that of the first example. In explaining addition of natural numbers, a primary schoolteacher had the following experience: when trying to explain to a child that $2+2=4$ by using the words "you have two apples and you are given another two, how many do you have then?", the pupil replied that he had no apples nor had anyone given him two more. The teacher tried to turn the difficulty by explaining in terms of other objects. But he did not succeed until by accident he hit upon a real circumstance in the child's experience by asking him to say how many pairs of shoes he had, and the reply came "one for Sundays and one for weekdays". Now he found it easy to elicit the fact that each pair consisted of two shoes making four in all.

(8) The example with 'envelopper' and the arithmetical one are related as follows: in the former case, the pupil remained *within the bounds of grammar*; in the latter, the child refused to *leave* language to *enter* grammar. (Here too we speak of grammar, since demonstrating the rules of arithmetic corresponds entirely to the treatment of verbs in the first example to demonstrating the rules of chess in the second.) The child simply cannot deal with number signs apart from the rest of language. It is this grammatical mode of treatment that is usually denoted by the expression 'formal science'. The words 'form' and 'content' were intended to mark the difference we have tried to explain through our examples.

(9) Having tried to explain what we understand by 'formal' – the treatment of signs within grammar in the widest sense – we return to the initial point of this chapter, that the language of science is a language that arose through more detailed treatment of some field. A further example of such treatment is the grammar of language itself, whether everyday or specialized. In modern symbolic logic (or logistic) for instance, certain operation words such as 'not', 'and', 'or', 'if', and so on have been taken from the fabric of ordinary language to become the object of a more specialised treatment. This forms the content of the 'calculus of propositions' (cf. Part Two, IV, 2). Likewise the 'theory of relations' is such a specialized treatment of relation words from ordinary language, like 'left', 'right', 'father', 'son', 'above', 'below', 'earlier', 'later', and so on. Such specialization further gives rise to new concepts, as in the case of the language of the sciences and the like. The language of conventional grammar has arisen from a specialization similar to that of the calculus of propositions and the theory of relations. (Under the heading of grammar we include the calculus of propositions, the theory of relations, parts of mathematics and of other fields, in short any mode of treatment that has for content the laying down and demonstrating of rules for the use of signs.) This 'differentiation' provokes distinctions that are not noticed at first, for example the distinction between the adjective 'fast' and the adverb 'fast'. The word 'adverb' was introduced to characterize this distinction and thus signifies it. Concern with language has led to a grouping of signs into 'parts of speech' and thus to formation of new signs (words) such as 'noun', 'verb', 'numeral' and so on. These words arise from a kind of specialization that we shall call grammatical. Just so, in the theory of relations, various words that denote properties of relations such as 'symmetrical', 'transitive', 'reflexive' and so on, were generated in this way.

(10) To sum up the discussion thus far, we observe two kinds of specialisation of language: (i) One that results in an extension of applied language, that is an adaptation of the vocabulary to the greater demands of life arising from more specialized concern with a given field, as happens in science. Such neologisms never relate to language, that is to the signs themselves, nor to their being different or combined with each other. (ii) A second that results in observing and formulating the existing multiplicity of language, while new terms are introduced to describe circum-

stances within it. (Hence this specialization like any others enriches the vocabulary: 'enrichment' always results from any specialization.) The words 'cardinal number' and 'ordinal number' are to *characterize* the difference between 'one' and 'first', but not introduce the signs 'one' and 'first' into the language for the purpose of operating; it is as it were a taking note or becoming aware that manifests itself in the description of the distinction between cardinal and ordinal number, that is in the introduction of just these words. 'Transitive' for example is a new coinage; it characterizes a feature common to the meaning of the words 'left', 'right', 'greater than', 'less than' and so on, in a way so far unnoticed. (If a is to the right of b and b to the right of c, then a is to the right of c; this property, which belongs to the meaning of the words 'left', 'right' and so on is called transitivity.) The emergence of words like 'time', 'number', 'word', 'meaning', 'negation', 'grammar', 'language', is an indication that the members of a language area have turned to the grammar of their language. Let these words be denoted as 'grammatical concepts'. (The failure to recognize the grammatical character of these concepts has led to very great misunderstandings.)

(11) These words produced by grammatical specialization may in turn become the object of further grammatical study: for instance one may consider the way the meaning of the word 'transitive' is related to that of 'reflexive' and so on, treating these words just like words of everyday life ('table', 'chair' and so on). Thus the words 'noun', 'verb' and so on, introduced for the sake of grammatical observations, are in their turn *inflected*. These words are incorporated into the vocabulary of those who are concerned with grammar and become part of their language, for they use these words with definite meanings and under definite rules of use. This use and these rules of use are laid down and discussed in a grammar; in short, they are used like any others.

CHAPTER III

OGIC AND GRAMMAR

1. Grammar of Material – Grammar of Meaning

(1) Large portions of conventional grammar may quite rightly be described as grammar of material, since we are there concerned only with the material of signs. This happens for example in phonetics, but also in morphology. The latter for instance is concerned with the various declensions: on the basis of material differences it makes distinctions and so creates schemata. For example, the two plural forms 'children' and 'dishes' differ only in that the first ends in *en* and the other in *es*. If one uses these two forms there is no difference in plural meaning over and above the difference of material. A *classification* by such differences concerns the acoustic difference between n and s or between the marks on paper. Similarly with the classification of verbs into strong and weak, for example sing, sang, sung, and paint, painted, painted. All these distinctions (differences in declension, conjugation, imperative mood and so on) were based on differences in material and have nothing to do with the signs' meanings. We can therefore say: grammar of material is involved wherever a material difference shows up in language without a corresponding semantic difference; such differences would not be recorded in a logical grammar. We have no wish to abolish these differences by intervening in the field of conventional grammar in order, for instance, to simplify (as Esperanto does). By 'critical grammar' we intend no reform of language whatsoever, but an examination of language as to semantic differences of its signs. For the grammar of meaning all material is equally suitable. (Of the two characteristics of Chinese the fact that the words are monosyllabic belongs to the grammar of material, while the positional indication of the word's relation to the sentence belongs to the grammar of meaning. The topic of this section would therefore have to figure in a critical grammar of Chinese.)

(2) The grammar of material may be compared with a book on chess that is unlike the usual ones in concentrating more on the externals of the

game, such as the appearance of the pieces and their consequent classification, with only occasional hints on moves and positions. What would
correspond to the grammar of meaning is a treatise on chess dealing
mainly with moves and positions while material is discussed only to the
extent that it is relevant to them.

(3) We might further imagine an art historian taking the trouble to
write a dissertation on the gradual development of the chess pieces in
different countries. (The form of the pieces is constantly changing as a
glance into an antique shop will show; besides, the form may 'exhibit'
various styles.) What corresponds to such treatment of chess pieces in the
case of language is generally called historical grammar.

(4) If the words 'nouns', 'adjectives', 'numerals' and so on had been
coined merely as collective terms to facilitate the learning of a language
and nothing else was meant by them, they would have nothing to do with
logic and would have to be regarded as one amongst many other equally
possible aids to language learning. However, grammatical classifications
have in fact a title to logical import. How far these terms express logical
circumstances and how far they capture non-logical matters we shall try
to show. (See Part Two, I, 3.)

2. ESSENTIAL AND UNESSENTIAL RULES IN GRAMMAR

(1) Before considering the case of language, let us see how one distinguishes between essential and inessential rules of a *game*.

(I) Suppose the rules of chess included the specification that the fields
must be squares and either black or white. If now we play a game and
notice that these rules do not affect the game so that any position on such
a board may be translated to one with rectangular fields that are red or
yellow, we say that these rules are inessential.

(II). There are rules that state that a pawn reaching the eighth rank
may be exchanged for any piece of the same colour except the king, or
that castling is subject to precise and defined conditions: these rules we
denote as essential, for without them *different positions* from the usual
ones could occur on the board. These rules belong to the 'meaning'
of the pieces, just as the rule that pawns move straight and take diago-
nally.

(2) Assume for a moment that we had to defend this view of essential

and inessential rules of chess against contrary views, and consider how we might go about our defence. For some one might assert that the rules under (I) and (II) are *equally essential* to chess, on the grounds that dropping any of these rules offends against the game ('chess' is made up of *all the rules*, even those under (I), on the present assumption) and that the game then played would not be chess, albeit very similar to it. But we can defend our views thus: take a board with red and yellow rectangular fields, contrary to rules (I), and on it *demonstrate a parallel game*, that is red and yellow here move like black and white there. We point to the fact that on both boards the same positions occur: if the queen is in check on one, then likewise on the other; if a bishop is threatened by a pawn on one, so it is on the other – in short any position whatever, considered to the last pro and con is the same in the two cases. Next we demonstrate the case where a rule of type (II) is not observed, again by playing a parallel game and showing that this leads to quite different positions, producing divergent positions in the two games. This pointing to the two cases is an appeal to the players to recognize the difference between rules that affect the game and ones that are more aesthetic or traditional in character.

This *appeal* is to be regarded as a *definition* of the concepts 'essential' and 'inessential', just as pointing to red light as 'red' and the verbal definition that explains a new and unknown sign in terms of old ones that are known. All are methods for ranging new signs into the fabric of language. If our language lacked facility for forming synonyms (so that *several* signs together often do the same job as another single sign: $A = B + C + D$), definition would be merely ostensive, or an appeal, without anyone ever demanding a verbal definition.

(3) If one regards language as a method of denoting, leaving out all other considerations, aesthetic, traditional or the like, then we observe in language circumstances quite similar to those we saw in chess. Let us therefore apply to language our findings from the model of chess: we note that a rule of logical grammar relates to the order of the terms a and b in sentences like 'a vanquished b', that inverting that order of the terms produces a different sentence. Another rule states that for example the sentence 'a is lying' and 'a mentions b' (intransitive and transitive verbs) differ in that one cannot say 'a is lying b' and 'a mentions'. To show that these are essential features of the language, let us examine what happens

if we ignore the order of terms in the relation '*a* beat *b*' (such sentences may be called relations; see Part Two, III, 12) or if we disregard the difference between transitive and intransitive verbs. The sentences '*a* beat *b*' and '*b* beat *a*' would have the same meaning, and besides one could say '*a* is lying *b*' and '*a* mentions'. The consequences correspond to those that ensue from ignoring rules (II) in chess, mentioned above. If however we omit another grammatical rule, like the distinction between weak and strong declension or conjugation mentioned in (1), this corresponds to modifications of chess resulting from changing the rules under (I). If I say 'dishen' instead of 'dishes', from the present point of view I merely offend against the conventional choice of material for plural endings. The meaning of the word and of the plural has nothing to do with it. To discover whether a rule is essential, one may construct a language that lacks this rule and then observe whether combinations of words (sentences) allowed in one are logically forbidden in the other, or vice versa. If so, then the rule is essential for the language that has it.

(4) Let us now show how these rules can be *read off* from a language, on the basis of facts observed in it. Consider for example the two sentences '*a* conquers *b*' and '*b* is conquered by *a*' one of these seems at first blush superfluous. (If we picture a situation like '*a* beats *b*', it makes no odds whether we say the picture means '*a* beats *b*' or '*b* is beaten by *a*'. Logically viewed, the passive form indicates the different position of the terms *a* and *b*. For if we invert their order in the active form, the original sentence is transformed into a different one. (There are relations where the terms can be interchanged without altering the sentence, for example '*a* is a cousin of *b*'. Not so for the word 'beat': that precisely is what the rule states.) Beside the active form language thus has another that specially marks this rule. (Or the reverse: one might take the active form as superfluous and as marking the rule of sequence. The only important point is that we can omit one of the two forms.) This rule for the position of *a* and *b*, which has its place somewhere in grammar, is expressed in the language itself: a special form has arisen in language to express this difference. We thus read off the rule from language by reflecting on the meaning of the passive and by observing the rule it expresses.

(5) The same purpose is here fulfilled by the accusative. For example in 'I beat *him*', the accusative marks the second term of the relation,

even if we invert the order as in 'him I beat'. The accusative form has the function of expressing the order of *a* and *b* by marking *b*.

However, in most cases in English there are no special accusative forms, yet the two expressions 'Caesar beat Ariovistus' and Ariovistus beat Caesar' do not mean the same. The order of the terms reveals itself in usage without special form and thus can be recorded in a grammatical rule.

(6) Consider now the rule about transitive and intransitive verbs, which does not manifest itself by special forms but still marks an important feature of our language. A special mode of applying signs has led grammar to make this distinction, which forbids expressions like '*a* is lying *b*' and '*a* mentions'. We say that the 'inhibitions' that arise when the forbidden expressions occur go back to an essential rule of grammar and that distinguishing between transitive and intransitive verbs means reading off a rule.

(7) This example diverges from the former firstly in that here the difference is not specially marked by special forms in language itself: whereas the rule of order is not a *prohibition*, using transitive verbs intransitively or vice versa is grammatically forbidden.

(8) Both rules here discussed concern *essential* features of our language, inasmuch as both for example belong to the meaning of the verb 'beat'. (The rules of use of 'beat' include both the rule that in '*a* beats *b*' we cannot omit *b*, and the order of *a* and *b* – the relation is asymmetrical. See Part Two, III, 12.)

3. GRAMMATICALLY AND LOGICALLY
UNOBJECTIONABLE SENTENCES

(1) So far we have shown (i) that some rules of grammar are also rules of logic and (ii) that others are not. We now want to show (iii) that ways of speaking that seem unobjectionable in the light of conventional grammar, logically speaking turn out to be senseless strings of signs and (iv) that ways of speaking that are logically unobjectionable may not be so in conventional grammar.

(2) As to (iii): We observe that such ways of speaking can arise only through neglect of essential rules, while all the rules of conventional grammar are obeyed – which shows that the latter is defective. We are

concerned with a series of prescriptions or prohibitions that show clearly in language but nevertheless were *not* recorded in grammar. Some have been brought to notice in books on logic, in mathematical logic and in various epistemological enquiries. Failure to obey them leads to so-called logical absurdities and to great confusion of thought. (Many rules to be discussed in Part Two belong to these prohibitions.) Ways of speaking generated in this way include the following, all unobjectionable in conventional grammar: 'I travel into the past', 'virtue is triangular', 'the leaf is willing' and so on. Conventional grammar admits all these, although they offend against logical grammar and ignore essential rules. (Using such sentences amounts to offending against the 'grammar of meaning'. This is evidently intended when we say that they offend against 'common sense', or that they are impossible ways of speaking. See Part Two, I, 5.)

(3) As to (iv), we observe that all prescriptions of the grammar of material (by which we are to understand all those areas of grammar that we have previously denoted as 'inessential') are logically irrelevant, as pointed out earlier. Ways of speaking can therefore be logically unobjectionable even if they break 'inessential' rules of grammar. The sentence 'the girl losed his own glove' contains *two* mistakes: the past tense of 'lose' is 'lost' and the possessive should be feminine; nevertheless the sentence is logically unobjectionable.

4. THE MOTIVE FOR INTRODUCING GRAMMATICAL DISTINCTIONS

(1) We earlier pointed to the need for introducing signs as a requirement of living and acting. For the sake of conveying information it was necessary to introduce signs such as 'river', 'game', 'timber', 'stone', 'fire'. With tribes that lived remote from the sea and lacked indirect contact as well (as for example through reports from others), there was evidently *no occasion* for introducing a sign such as 'sea'.

(2) The formation of the distinctions in the use of signs that are set down in grammar, derives likewise from *motives* in actual life: the quite different situation of victor and vanquished for example requires the coining of a sentence form in which the terms cannot be arbitrarily interchanged. (If there were an idiom such that '*a* vanquishes *b*' and '*b* vanquishes *a*' meant the same, the sign 'vanquishes' would not be

the same as ours, for it would mean that one of the two vanquished the other; its meaning covers that of our sign only in part and could not express what we want to know, namely who beat whom.) Just so, the affairs of life, led to the formation of different words such as he, she and so on. Similarly, the difference between one individual and several of them (perhaps in hunting or fighting) led to different forms that grammarians call 'singular' and 'plural'. The making up of different forms for events of the past and for ones that will presumably have occurred in the future, goes back to the need for profiting from memories and setting oneself goals. Our language is of course not closed: new motives can and may lead to new distinctions that will be laid down in grammar after the event.

(3) Let us consider an example where actual life provides a motive that rarely occurs at present but nevertheless seems obvious. There might be many departments of life in which certain elements of a domain are ranged in threes. Domains of pairs are well known (two eyes, ears, hands, feet), a fact duly recorded in the *dual* forms in certain languages. A language that goes further and acts on the motive for triplets would in addition evolve special forms for groups of three. Motives of this kind thus lead to the making up of various words and word systems. The various uses of words in language for their part led the grammarian to introduce his special language or terminology.

(4) These reflections make us see that such motives may well result in different forms (passive, active, past, future and so on), but they give no clue as to the introduction of strong and weak conjugations: the cause why different materials are used for the same meaning is not explained. Let us now introduce a way of speaking to make this difference more precise: grammatico-logical distinctions (differences within the grammar of meaning) go back to *inducements*; while the choice of certain materials, and in particular of different materials for the same purpose, has its *causes*.

(5) There is no inducement for marking certain things as masculine and others as feminine. If a certain tribe imagines the sun as a man and moon as a woman, then sun and moon are grammatically on the same level as man and woman, which gives occasion for Latin Sol (masculine) and Luna (feminine). Of the suggestion here, as in the opposite case of German '*der* Mond' (masculine) and '*die* Sonne' (feminine) for example,

we may say that it has been *lost*, so that these forms are observed in languages from tradition only. (The inducement and occasion may be lost, leaving the form behind. If changed circumstances then lead to a corresponding reform, they have *occasioned* it.) Without wishing to suggest reform, we can say that the inducement for distinguishing masculine from feminine might best be met by introducing three genders (masculine, feminine and neuter), the last one answering the need to mark off those things that belong to neither of the other two ('natural gender', see 5, gender).

(6) In the languages current in our parts we have a first, second and third person (personal pronouns). This distinction arose because it was important to separate the speaker from the spoken to, or from some other about whom we are speaking. There are many situations in everyday life where it is vital to keep these apart, and so the distinction has stamped itself on language. Here we must consider two points: (i) One might think that whether or not a language distinguish between first, second and third persons, a man has a certain feeling of his own person (for example familiarity, or a concept of his own body, and the like); whereas he feels differently towards others (for example strangeness, and the like). (ii) On the other hand, it might be precisely such grammatical distinctions that provoke feelings of similar kinds. If the former, then feelings may have contributed to the formation of grammatical distinctions like I – you – he. But we must still distinguish the function of these signs in language from the suggestion that has occasioned their introduction: the distinction between meaning and inducement. What makes me buy chairs and tables for my room is not the same as the function of these objects in my room. If the latter, the feelings that arose after introduction of the signs 'I – you – he' and so on (which, we know from experience, differ for different people) have just as little to do with the function of these signs within language. It may well be that somebody seeing certain objects in my room will thereby experience all kinds of associations from memory without this having any bearing on the use of these objects. Language, which is tied in with the most varied human activities and feelings, owes its form and distinctions to whatever led people to introduce them, but can in turn provoke certain feelings. Studying the needs that have occasioned linguistic form, or the feelings and imagination set off by it, is not the business of grammar.

5. GREATER OR SMALLER REPERTOIRE OF LINGUISTIC FORMS

(1) We proceed to a closer look at the grammar of meaning as to the various distinctions made in it on the basis of factual findings. What strikes us here is that various languages of the type of ours exhibit different distinctions, and these with different degrees.

(2) To capture these differences correctly, consider a few models: one might for example imagine a language in which the conventional degrees of comparison (positive, comparative, superlative, as in bright, brighter, brightest) are replaced by another scheme. As to the logical significance of these terms, note that 'bright' applies to all shades of brightness, insofar as we are not concerned to mark differences in the field within which we use 'bright'; we are concerned with the system: bright – dark. But as positive term in the threefold system 'bright' means the lowest element of the field (the one that is not brighter than another). For here 'bright' is intended as contrast to 'brighter': the comparative applies to all shades of an arbitrarily delimited field except a lowest element. (The opposite 'less bright' applies to all elements of a field except a specific highest element.) All this so long as the comparative contrasts with the positive; if 'brighter' belongs to the threefold system it excludes the highest element as well. The superlative signifies the recognition of the highest elements of such a field and cannot be applied to any other of its elements. We may now conceive two possibilities:

(I) *Increasing the number of forms.* This might occur for example from the following motive: suppose we often had to cross four rooms that differ mainly in brightness, corresponding to different methods of lighting: room B is more brightly lit than room A, C more brightly than B and D than C (cf. analogous situations in trying out spectacles). The sentences (i) 'B brighter than A', (ii) 'C brighter than B', (iii) 'D brighter than C', and (a) 'C brighter than A', (b) 'D brighter than B', (c) 'D brighter than A' express the fact that one room is brighter than the other. Differences in brightness that have to be rendered by our comparative here require *two sentences* combined; for example C is brighter than B and B than A, in contrast both with (i) – (iii) and (a) – (c). However, these circumstances might have suggested a system in which grammarians recognize five degrees of comparison (three comparatives): in such a language the above differences in brightness could be rendered by *one* sentence.

(II) *Decreasing the number of forms.* Suppose the superlative were missing and we had only positive and comparative: we lack the means of marking the highest element of a field. This would not alter the meaning of 'bright' as against 'dark' nor against 'brighter': but the comparative of this twofold system without an upper bound does not exclude the superlative – 'brighter' is not opposed to 'brightest'. The differences considered here are not to be equated with what we earlier called inessential rules of language, since it is not a question of use of material, but of certain inducements for extending or restricting the multiplicity of forms.

(3) Consider one more example. Suppose some language confined itself to the numerals '1', '2', '3' and 'several'. Comparing this with our ordinary language, we observe first of all that 'several' occurs there too. The hypothetical language cannot distinguish between 4, 5, 6 and so on, and is therefore poorer than our language precisely by these signs, which are the means for expressing these differences. As to the signs 1, 2, 3 the rules are the same in both cases. We might therefore feel inclined to say that the smaller multiplicity does not affect the meaning of already existing signs, since these last obey the same rules. However, this is a mistake: the sign '2' in our own language can for example be explicated by $2+2=4$ or $2\times2=4$ and so on, which belong to the sign's meaning: while the sign '2' of the model can be explicated only by $1+1$ and $3-1$ (provided addition and subtraction apply, although they would themselves have different significance here). This diminution in forms would produce essential changes in the number system of our language.

(4) Before proceeding to further examples, let us emphasize the general point that *there is no upper bound to multiplicity.* Thus there might be not just three, or five, degrees of comparison, but as many as you like, leading to quite new distinctions and grammatical systems of which we have no idea.

(5) *Gender.* Let us consider how we might extend or restrict multiplicity here. Assume for simplicity that the previously mentioned rule concerning natural gender had been implemented. After such a reform the distinction between masculine and feminine could mean no more than emphasis of the difference (which shows in pronouns) where desired. (The neuter might be designed to separate the living from the inanimate.

It thus would forbid certain substitutions. One could say 'he or she wants' but not 'it wants'. However, this 'neuter' would belong to another grammatical system that might consist of three 'genders': (1) all inanimate things, (2) all living things except man, (3) all human animals. Thus the verb 'to think' could not go with a noun of the first gender – the gender would forbid it. For this mode of classification there would be an important motive. In what follows we shall use gender to refer only to masculine and feminine.) One can conceive a language whose pronouns show no distinctions in gender; for example, the word 'this' applies to all genders: from a sentence containing it we could not infer differences between masculine and feminine. 'This' is equivalent to the German 'dieser, diese, dieses' without the explicit differences of gender. Similarly for all other pronouns. Conversely, Hebrew has more marked distinctions of gender in its personal pronouns. For example 'you' when addressed to a woman is 'ath', to a man 'atha'. Such a distinction might equally well be imagined for the first person. This would constitute a linguistic gain as to scope for expressing differences in gender. All this shows that such differences may be either disregarded, or emphasized by special forms, as would for example appear if we opened a book and saw a sentence containing 'you': if it is in Hebrew, we can infer from the personal pronoun whether a woman or a man is spoken to; if in English, only context will tell. We regard the loss of difference as inessential: if 'he' and 'she' were everywhere replaced by a 'neutral' word, the affected sentences, though poorer (that is, their analyses would lack the sentence 'x is a man' or 'x is a woman'), would never become devoid of sense. But that, too, goes back to the suggestion that most states, actions, and so on, can be predicated of man and woman alike. Since no substitutions are barred, the distinction becomes inessential.

(6) *Number*. Imagine a language without plural and numerals. Although there is strong motive for creating these forms, assume that no distinction is made between 'one' and 'many', or 'man' (A) and 'men' (A, B and C). From the point of view of our own, developed language, we would describe a speaker of this hypothetical one as applying, for instance, the word 'lion' to one and many without noticing the difference. We may of course suppose that if time and again he saw one lion and then two or several together he would discover the plural – that is, find his way towards a language with plural; but let us keep to our assumption.

Comparing his language with ours we observe that his is the poorer by much: for one thing many sentences of ours cannot be expressed in his. As to rules of use for words in the two languages, the words of his language lack precisely the rules of the plural.

(7) Imagine further a language with numerals and plurals but without ordinal numbers. Although one cannot now form 'fourth' from 'four', the word 'four' would retain its meaning; that is, it would be applicable wherever we use our word 'four', but it would be impossible to denote the order of the counted objects. (In this language 'four' could not be explained in contrast with 'fourth'. One could not say that the order of the counted objects did not matter.) This would mean a reduction in multiplicity.

(8) Next, imagine a language possessing a greater multiplicity as to number. Suppose there were different forms for 'one' depending on whether it was 'one of two', 'one of three', 'one of four' or 'one of several' (cf. in part African class languages). Likewise for ordinals, that is 'the first of two', 'the first of three' and so on. Moreover, let there be corresponding plural forms for nouns, that is duals, forms for triplets, quartets and so on. (Such forms would consistently carry through the merging of noun with number that begins with the plural.) The reader can construct further complications by himself. Comparing this language with ours, we observe that our word 'two' (or 'second' contains the meaning of all the others (two of 2, 4, 5 and so on) but is poorer in differentiation. Analogously for the plural. To express 'two of three' in our language one must use precisely these three words, whereas the hypothetical language has one definite cardinal form for it.

(9) As with gender and number so in other cases, for instance tense (cf. languages without simple future or pluperfect; or we may imagine languages richer than our own).

(10) Ordinals, cardinals (both ours and the special kinds imagined) plural, gender, tense, threefold pronouns and so on will be called *operational systems*. Language is not only a reservoir of signs (it contains not only systems of signs for colours, activities and so on), but also of operational systems. In Chapter I we set up two criteria for distinguishing between less and more developed languages. By the second criterion a language is the more developed to the extent that it has operators that enable a great many sentences to be formed with the given signs. Numerals,

for instance, are such operators: they make possible the formation of many sentences in this sense. Likewise with tenses, comparison and so on: by means of the words 'after', 'before', 'more' (to which the relevant inflections correspond) they give rise to many sentences. In forming plurals, comparisons or tenses, one uses the same words ('lion', 'big', 'walk' and so on) in a well defined manner.

(11) These reflections lead to the following insight: a language has greater multiplicity, or is 'richer', if it has more operational systems than some other language (if the number of operational systems is the same, what counts is their degree of development). A language with fewer operational systems has smaller multiplicity, it is 'poorer'.

6. The pre-grammatical stage of language

(1) If an adult tells a child 'this is a stone', in order first to attract its attention to the presence of the stone, but then also to explain how the word 'stone' is used, and he notices the difference between the two sentences, we can say that he has become aware of the nature of grammar. But if he cannot see the difference, we speak of a *state devoid of grammar*. For us, who have already been made aware of grammatical distinctions and can distinguish between something laid down to explain a sign on the one hand and an assertion on the other, this could be described by saying that the two sentences belong to different grammatical types (see Part Two, III). Since our hypothetical adult does not know this distinction, we can say that from his point of view the language is devoid of grammar. When a philologist observes that Bantu languages have certain rules, this does not mean that the Bantu themselves must observe this, but that in a certain way we read off the grammar of their language.

(2) Within our own language, too, we can distinguish areas in which assertions are made, commands given, desires voiced and so on; but the words there used do not reveal any awareness of grammar. Such areas can be described as devoid of grammar.

(3) Grammar may be pursued in two ways: (1) according to a kind of *legislation*, that is we lay down what rules are to hold; (2) through *observation* of existing rules. On the one hand we fix norms, on the other we register existing rules. Fixation and consequent use occurs already in the grammarless state; but reading off is a matter of grammar. This

includes the construction of models, that is the presentation of a possible use of signs according to freely chosen rules. In this one makes trial use of possible legislation.

(4) It is commonly said that language is older than grammar. From our point of view, if grammar is the laying down and following of certain rules, then it exists wherever there is language at all. But if by grammar we mean an awareness of the nature of language, the pursuit of grammar, the emergence of certain terms that go back to grammatical awareness, then it lies in the nature of linguistic development that such activities begin only when language has reached a fairly developed state.

CHAPTER IV

LOGIC AND PSYCHOLOGY

1. PSYCHOLOGISM

(1) Logic and psychology are both concerned with 'thought': psychology, besides dealing with feeling, sensation and so on, deals with thinking; while logic deals exclusively with 'thought' and its laws. For this reason, logic used to be construed as part of psychology.

(2) The relation between logic and psychology was regarded as similar to that of economic geography to geography as such. In geography, one does indeed deal with economic geography, but not as thoroughly as in the special subject and without the help of other external theories such as economics. Just so it was held that the task of logic was to deal with thought, in a specialist way on the one hand, and with the help of general philosophic theories (external to psychology) on the other. But since psychology is a natural science, that is one of the sciences that describe the course of external events and discuss their regularities, the laws of logic (or thought) were regarded as laws of nature. (The concept 'law' is ambiguous and misleading: we speak of political, moral, natural and logical laws, a linguistic ambiguity producing much misunderstanding. The tendency was to liken the laws of thought to those of physics rather than those of government, although the latter would be more appropriate.)

(3) The underlying train of thought is this: just as any physical law is obtained by observing certain connections in a number of instances, so too are the 'laws of logic'. This approach, appearing more or less clearly in various treatises on logic is usually called psychologism.

2. ON THE REFUTATION OF PSYCHOLOGISM

(1) Since historically this prejudice has led to a mistaken view of logic and goes on enticing people into this mistake, it seems necessary to refute the position by means of some examples, at the same time consolidating those views already attained regarding the nature of logic.

(2) Let us therefore consider four examples from different fields, four possibilities that could violently shake our ordinary views.

(i) Suppose one day we had the following experience: bodies normally expected to fall to the ground when released, suddenly rise.

(ii) If we have always seen two objects together, we are accustomed on meeting one of them to remember the other spontaneously: suppose then that this expected memory were not to come up.

(iii) According to a well known rule of logical deduction, all men are mortal and Caius is a man entail that Caius is mortal. Suppose that someone who knows all these words well and always uses them correctly declared one day that the third sentence did not follow from the first two. Imagine we found this not only with one person but with a whole group.

(iv) We observe some chessplayers with whom we have played several times before so that we have satisfied ourselves as to their precise grasp of the rules of chess: now we find them moving rooks the same way as bishops.

(3) In all four cases we should be rather astonished for a start. Let us now examine how we should try to explain the several modes of curious behaviour.

In case (i), which concerns the validity of a physical law, we should say: the law that held till now, based on a series of observations that bodies when released fall to the ground, does not hold always and everywhere. This would be quite a conceivable state of affairs, and would demand precisely this sort of explanation. In case (ii), which concerns the psychological. law of association, one would try a similar sort of explanation, for this too is a natural law and thus obtained on the basis of experience on which alone it rests.

In case (iii) we are concerned with the way 'all' is used. Evidently Caius comes under 'all men' and if it holds of all men that they are mortal, then of Caius too. We shall therefore ask these people what they mean by 'all men'. Perhaps they mean that assertions about 'all men' allow of exceptions. But if they deny this and keep to the usual meanings of the other words as well but still maintain that Caius was not mortal, we should be forced to assume that these people are incapable of orderly speech, that is they cannot obey the rules for 'all' that they *themselves* have laid down. This inability of theirs would *not alter* the rules that hold for 'all' and so on, since these same people have expressly acknowledged these rules, using them correctly in other cases. Similarly in case (iv): we should start by asking them what rules are to govern rook and bishop. If they told or showed us the usual rules and still occasionally moved a rook like a bishop, the rules, as above, would remain the same for them, but their mode of playing would be confused. But if they named other rules, which allowed the rook additional scope to move like a bishop, this would simply be a different game (see III, 2) and not ordinary chess.

(4) As we have seen, the for examples can be divided into *two* groups: the experiences in (i) and (ii) lead to a change in the natural laws that apply: we should have to give up the existing laws of physics and psychology; in (iii) and (iv) this does not arise: we say rather that people speak *incorrectly* or play *wrongly*, if they accept the usual rules of language or chess, or they speak *another* language or play *another* game, if they replace the usual rules by others. For the so-called laws of logic (such as the above rule of inference) are not laws of nature: they do not indicate the regularity of thought, but are comparable rather to the rules laid down for a game. The laws of psychology on the other hand (like the law of association) are quite comparable with the laws of physics.

(5) A well known law in logical grammar is the 'law of contradiction'. It states, to use an example, that if I say: 'it is raining here and now' (with precise place and time) I cannot at the same time assert that it is not raining here and now. It is not as though 'cannot' meant that we find it hard to conceive a state in which it is both raining and not raining. With habits of thought that have become second nature, and as it were 'necessary', we can always ignore certain circumstances and thus free ourselves from those habits. Here it is different: as long as we adopt a language in which 'not' and 'and' are operators that are used in certain ways revealed in use, we 'cannot' assert the two sentences 'it is raining' and 'it is not raining' together at once – it contradicts the rules we have laid down for combining signs. (If someone has decided not to smoke, he cannot then smoke and keep his resolution.)

(6) Every sentence in science or daily life presupposes this law (or rule) of contradiction, because every sentence can be denied and sentences can be linked by 'and'. Psychology is a science like physics, chemistry or geography and so on, except that it treats of certain processes in man, while the others deal with other parts of the world. Psychology like any

other science expresses its findings in assertions or surmises, and these presuppose the rule of contradiction. Psychology and the other sciences simply presuppose that our speech and thought is not confused and disorderly, or that certain rules must be obeyed: that is what is logical about them.

(7) Without logical rules, nothing could be asserted. Even when a primitive man says to another (or conveys by gesture or merely thinks to himself): there lies a stone and not a stick, he 'calculates', from our point of view, with an orderly language containing general names, numbers, conjunctions and negations; if he wants to say or think something, he cannot do it without observing certain rules. For nothing can be said or thought that does not obey certain rules. Where there are no rules there are no assertions either.

(8) In contrast with psychology, logic does not deal with processes in a definite district of the world, and is therefore not confined to any (spatio-temporal) region. If I pronounce the familiar form of the rule of inference 'if p, then q; p, therefore q' this holds for things in the room or in the street, on our planet or beyond the solar system. It is merely a rule laid down about 'if' and 'then', nothing more. Once I introduce these words with the meanings that appear in the above formula, it is valid 'necessarily' everywhere and everywhen, that is precisely so long as the words have the meanings thus given to them. While logic is thus concerned with the rules of language and is unlimited as to time and place, psychology describes and explains processes concerning the earth's humans (ordinary psychology) or animals (animal psychology) or groups (mass psychology) and so on.

(9) A rule of logic *holds* until repealed: a law of psychology however is considered as *holding* until we observe evidence to the contrary. In this sentence the verb 'to hold' is used twice, but it is easy to see that there is ambiguity here, just as in the sentences

(a) x is *held* to be honest,
(b)   the rule of driving on the left *holds* in England.

In (a) *to hold* means that x is known to behave in certain ways and will presumably go on doing so, while (b) indicates that a rule to drive on the left has been laid down (and is in fact obeyed). The *holding* of psychological laws corresponds to (a), that of logical laws to (b).

(10) Logic deals also with signs that can be clearly shown not to belong to psychology. Certain words, whose treatment in logic plays a considerable part, namely 'and', 'not', 'or', 'if' and so on, evidently do not correspond to any sensations or ideas. They are only operators, whose meaning is fixed through their use.

(11) One of the best known definitions of logic states that it is the theory of correct thinking. If one gains correct insight into the nature of logic, one can equally say that it is the theory of correct speaking, or writing and so on. One is easily misled into confusing logic with psychology. To grasp the correct distinction, one must clarify the matter by means of examples until one sees that it is really self-evident. (A discussion of psychologism is found in the works of *Frege* and *Husserl*.)

(12) We compare the rules of logic with those of a game, insofar as their infringement alters the symbolic 'meaning' of the pieces; or with moral, social or political laws, insofar as one can speak about all of them in terms of obeying or not obeying, but not of truth and falsehood.

(13) Logical rules differ essentially from technical advice relating to the use of tools of every kind. The technical side of scientific research does not belong to logic either, but must be compared rather with that of navigation and so on. *Mill's* system of inductive logic and his methods of research belong to the researcher's guide book, but not to the list of rules of language; his advice on observations and experiment do not lay down meanings nor contain linguistic prohibitions - such advice belongs rather to the technical side of actions, to the application of language and not to an examination of language itself. (The logical aspect of such examinations are grammatical examinations of the concepts 'induction', 'hypothesis', 'law', 'observation' and so on.)

(14) For logic, examination of the grammar of say, an African language and that of the language of a science are equivalent. For all linguistic systems offer examples for grammatical observations. But the obtaining and application of knowledge is as little a part of logic as the description of primitive techniques of nutcracking.

3. Psychologistic interpretation of words

(1) We have already aquainted ourselves with the fact that some words are used with many meanings; in particular certain words have one

meaning in everyday language and another in the language of science. There is a series of words whose meanings in psychology are different from those in everyday language (apart from their multiple meaning even there). These are the words: 'I', 'understand', 'know' and so on. Grammatically speaking, these words should be treated as part of a systematic treatment of all the signs of a language. However we shall discuss them here because they are especially liable to lead to a psychologistic interpretation. To clarify the different use of certain words in the language of psychology, suppose we imagine several experimental subjects were asked about their ideas of 'I'. When one of them answers 'I have such and such an idea', he will clearly not have considered whether on uttering the first word of his answer he had just this very idea that for him holds as criterion for using the word. Likewise for the psychologist who asked the question; the word 'I' that he will adopt in the later stages of his researches in the way that the results indicate is simply used to mean these ideas (or what is common to them); but not so in his other uses of language. The difference between the two meanings may be put thus: the ordinary 'I' is a personal pronoun, the 'I' of the ego ideas of each subject and of the psychologist is a general name for experiences (this presupposes certain clarifications about personal pronouns and general names; see Part Two, II).

(2) The meaning of such words in contexts more specially concerned with mental experience differs from their meaning in everyday language (including all science except these very parts of psychology). Thus, if a professor of psychology asks 'Have you understood my explanations about the understanding?' he uses two languages in the one sentence; 'understanding' is meant in the special sense of psychology, the results that the psychologists gathers from his experimental subjects; but 'understood' is used in its everyday meaning.

(3) An example will bring out the two different meanings intended here. Suppose a teacher is trying to impart some sentence or concept of mathematics. On having explained it he asks whether the pupils are now familiar with the concept and one of them says no. The teacher then tries again to explain using the pedagogic means at his disposal and finally the pupil exclaims: 'Ah, now I understand.' By this he may mean: 'I now have the feeling that I always have when I come to grasp something', thus pointing to the moment of enlightenment. Suppose the

teacher is interested in psychology and questions the pupil somewhat as follows: 'What did you experience at that moment, can you still retain and render it?' But perhaps the pupil is not attuned to self-observation, so that he could hardly report on his own experience, seeing that what he was concentrating on was not his own psychic processes but the objective meaning of the concept and its application. Can the teacher say of this pupil, who is unable to report on the *process* of understanding, that he had failed to understand the concept in question? Clearly not, for the ordinary word 'understand' does not aim at a certain kind of experience or its description. If we want to find out whether somebody has understood something, we ask for test cases of his having understood, that is we observe whether he knows how to use the concept or sentence according to common usage (or according to the rules that apply in the field concerned, for instance mathematics). We test whether somebody has understood the words 'to the left of' by asking him to indicate situations in which he would use the words, for example 'Charing Cross station lies to the left of Trafalgar Square if you come out of the National Gallery'. We say that somebody has understood a concept if it has been integrated into the rest of his language, if it has been given a place in the linguistic fabric. The understanding of a concept or sentence is this integration into the linguistic system.

(4) One often speaks of understanding more or better, for instance pupil A has understood a sentence or word better than pupil B. This clearly does not mean that A on being confronted with the word or sentence has more lively ideas than B. Rather, it is a case of words often being ambiguous (as already explained) as well as now vague and now more precise, and of sentences at first blush simple turning out to be composite and so on. It is a matter of understanding greater or smaller parts of the concept's meaning, more or fewer clauses of the sentence in question, and the like. Such degrees of understanding show in the way a user employs these items more or less readily.

(5) *Knowing*. Since the word 'to know' is sometimes not accurately distinguished from 'to understand' which has just been explained, let us notice a definite difference in meaning. The meaning of 'understand' in certain sentences may be described thus: to understand a concept or sentence is to integrate it with the linguistic system. We speak of knowing (leaving aside other meanings) when we are concerned with the truth

or falsehood of one or more sentences. A sentence beginning with 'I know...' is an indicative assertion (see Part Two III,2). For example, I know that it is raining (or not raining), or in general, that this or that is true or false. But one cannot say 'I understand that it is raining' in the relevant sense (although the sentence has a use, with the main verb meaning 'I am informed'). Thus we can apply knowing to ignorance, as in 'I know that I do not know whether...', '... why ...' and the like; but not 'I understand that I do not understand a certain sentence'. Note that if understanding refers to a sentence, one may well understand what is false. For example I can understand the false sentence 'this book is bigger than that one', while knowing it to be false. But if I *know* that the sentence is false I can no longer *know* that it is true. For if I *know* it to be true, I know that it, and not its opposite, holds. If one understands a positive sentence, one understands also its negative. But not so with knowing. It strikes us that 'know' is often followed by 'that'; while 'understand' is usually not, and if it is, the word 'understand' is loosely used as in 'I understand that you did not come', meaning 'I have been told...'. In such cases, understanding is not integrating concepts or sentences into the linguistic system. The difference between 'understand' and 'know' may be put thus: the former relates to an aquaintance with the system of signs, the latter presupposes such aquaintance.

(6) The following example is to make plain the confusion of psychologism. 'I know that there is somebody in the next room'. This sentence is not to express a conjecture, but merely to describe a feeling or state of mind, roughly in the sense of 'I have a presentiment'. Assume the person who thus expressed his state of mind is led into the next room where he becomes convinced that no one is there. We could now ask him two sorts of question: (i) 'did you actually have a feeling that someone was there?' (ii) 'Is your assertion true?' (because his feeling became an assertion). Assuming that he is always very correct in his answers, he would reply as follows (i) 'I actually had the feeling' and (ii) 'the assertion is false, there is no one there'. The two replies are quite compatible, for one speaks of a mental state and the other of the presence of somebody in the next room. Let us now vary the case. The man says 'I know that there is somebody in the next room', 'I know' being used in the usual sense as relating to truth. If now we took him to the next room as before, he could reply to only one of the two questions, namely by retracting his

previous assertion: he would have to say that *his previous knowing* was erroneous and his assertion false.

(7) In the light of these few examples, intended to explain the psychologistic confusion of meanings, the reader may reflect similarly on the use of words like 'remember', 'error', 'lie', 'belief', 'doubt'.

PART TWO

ON THE GRAMMAR OF WORDS, SENTENCES AND COMBINATIONS OF SENTENCES

CONTENTS OF PART TWO

(1) From our preliminary enquiry into the nature of logic and the relation between grammar and psychology in Part One, we now proceed to explain the structure of our ordinary language by means of examples.

(2) Part Two is divided into four chapters. Chapter I, headed 'General remarks', will deal with various topics that crop up in the literature of logic and grammar, such as definition, intonation, metaphor and so on. Some of these appear in logic texts, others in grammars.

(3) The three subsequent chapters: II. Kinds of words, III. Kinds of sentences, IV. Combinations of sentences, relate to the difference, important in our language, between word, sentence and combination of sentences. (Traditional logic has analogous divisions, concept, judgment, inference. What follows will show that judgments, or assertions, are only *one* type of sentence, and that inference likewise is only one type of combination of sentences.) We must emphasize that this mirrors only the structure of *our* language, to forestall the natural mistake of regarding this division as being somehow necessary: this is not the case. Any actual or imagined language with their most varied structures, whether or not divided like ours above, may become objects of logical study insofar as the rules that can be read off can be observed and recorded. Our language merely has the advantage that we are acquainted with it. We therefore use mainly the language of every day because we all know it: from it we shall select a more or less vague slice to demonstrate a variety of rules.

(4) In Chapter II the partly misleading division of words into nouns, verbs and the like is retained because most people are acquainted with it and because given the complexity of language no division would satisfy all substitution rules (see Part Two, I, 3). It was therefore found preferable to indicate the differences within the traditional word groupings.

(5) In Chapter III, only those sentence types are discussed that occur most often in everyday language. Every grammar deals with prototypes of words and sentences. All types of words and sentences in currency

are there represented by examples. It goes without saying that the needs of human life produce other types of sentences (or might do so) – as to that, there are no bounds to linguistic formations.

(6) Chapter IV deals with certain combinations of sentences, amongst them traditional inferences of logic and the combinations by means of logical constants that are treated in symbolic logic. These are very interesting as examples, so long as they claim no monopoly over all speech and thought but are regarded merely as the grammar of certain signs. However, we shall guard against any despotic subjugation of the *whole* of language.

CHAPTER I

GENERAL REMARKS

1. THE DIVERSITY OF WORDS

(1) To learn what we understand by the diversity of the words of a language, let us look at an imaginary method of learning certain words like 'red', 'green', 'before', 'and' taken as paradigms. The scheme is moreover to focus attention on the point at which imitation stops and use begins, where the sounds become *words*.

(2) Imagine a room in which two lights are suspended each provided with a device for lighting up a number of colours (green, red, yellow and so on) successively and at will. An adult in this room is to teach a child the words 'red', 'green', 'before', 'and', by using the lights. Step (i) One light shows red several times in succession while each time the teacher says 'red', asking the child to do likewise. Whenever the light shines, the child now says 'red', even if the teacher no longer does (We could equally bring the child to say 'green' to a red light, but that would be teaching him to use what in our language is incorrect material.)

Step (ii) The teacher now lets the light shine green, repeating the first step except for saying 'green' instead of 'red', practising the move until error seems impossible.

Step (iii) Now the teacher shines the lamp variously: red, green, several reds, several greens and so on without any definite rule of sequence and the child is to say the correct word each time.

Step (iv) The light which so far always gave the same shade of red – say vermilion – is now shone in different shades: purple, carmine and so on. The child is taught to say red to all these.

Step (v) The same is done with different shades of green.

Step (vi) Now the lamp is made to shine in the rhythm green – red – pause. Teacher and child say 'green *before* red'.

Step (vii) The same as (vi), but interchanging the colours.

Step (viii) Till now, only one light was used. Now the teacher lets them shine both together one green and the other red, while saying 'green *and* red'.

We now repeat (i) – (viii) with other pairs of colours, for which we use indices for greater clarity: *a* for blue-yellow, *b* for white-violet and so on.

At step (viii) *b* a sufficiently intelligent child may spontaneously say 'white *and* violet'. What is important is that it spontaneously and correctly applies words (here 'and') to cases it has not learnt directly. It is conceivable that the teacher must start afresh in each case, but notice that the ability to use a language in a variety of cases consists precisely in this spontaneous ability to apply words to other cases.

(3) When the child first uses the sign 'and' (or 'before' in (vi) *x*) and even when spontanously applying it to other cases, his sign 'and' (or 'before') is far from identical with ours. We might say that his 'and' and 'before' are tacitly defined only as applying to *definite* cases. (In speaking of 'words' here it is clear that we cannot be using the sign in the way we do when normally speaking about words of our language: for the meaning of its words includes the mode of use *in sentences* that children at this stage are not yet acquainted with. It has been said that a language can consist of mere words, but these cannot be the words of our language, whose meaning includes precisely the rules of use in sentences.)

(4) We now let the lights shine as follows: one of them in the sense of 'red before green' with the usual pause, and the second in the sense of 'green before red'. If now the child forms the expression 'green before red *and* red before green', thus showing its ability to use 'and' here too, then he has extended the word 'and' by a further rule: the word, at first used only for single pairs (in (viii), *a*, *b*... *x*), is now applied also to sequences of pairs.

(5) Assume now that the child extends his vocabulary by learning the use of the words 'hard', 'soft', 'cold', 'warm'. The grammar of his word 'and' is then further completed if he can apply 'and' to 'white and cold' (when seeing and touching snow, similar situations arise on seeing fire in a stove: red and warm; or grass: soft and green). The possibility of application to *two* senses is an advance here, covering a new partial domain of meaning (new rules of use). When we speak of partial domains of a language or a sign this evidently relates to the vocabulary existing in the language community or to the current mode of application of the sign; for there is no ideal language with fixed boundaries, nor ideal meanings of single signs.

(6) This learning model is of course quite remote from what actually happens in learning. We can compare the two processes with different ways in which a drawing may take shape. One might imagine that the artist draws separate distinct and individually recognizable objects which together make up the picture: first a table, then a bench, then a picture on the wall and so on. Alternatively he might draw a few strokes here and a few there which are not separately intelligible, and only towards the end, when a lot has been done, can we recognize the connections and thus the picture as a whole. The model corresponds to the former, the actual learning process rather to the latter.

(7) As to the model: to illustrate a word's meaning one can give only examples, the further application must be carried out by the user himself. 'Carry out oneself' here means to observe how certain words are used and then to use them in the same way in similar cases. This requires a peculiar focusing of the attention which occurs more or less consciously whenever we read about a subject so far unknown to us. It becomes quite conscious when we improve our grasp of a foreign language in the country where it is spoken.

(8) We begin to be able to apply words at the point where we progress from mechanical imitation to understanding. This ability to apply is important because mere imitation, that is repetition of speech sounds, does not yet involve signs, words, meanings and so on; only afterunderstanding the word 'red', that is when the child can operate with the word on his own, can we speak of a *word* (with the previously mentioned restrictions that apply to the child's word). If in step (i) he has learnt to say 'red' on his own when the light shines and to use the word whenever the light shines vermilion, we can already speak of a usage even if the child does not extend the word to purple red objects. (Someone might for instance have learnt to use numbers in connection with people, fruit or objects in general, without extending them to events, times, spaces, behaviour and the like. He would then speak of two men but not of two cases of death, two hours and the like.)

(9) *From the observer's point of view* the child having reached this stage should be able to say: "At one time the teacher in a similar situation said 'red' and evidently wanted me to do likewise whenever such a light appears, therefore I shall articulate the sound 'red' in all such cases". (The child, for his part, does not have this thought, since it cannot operate

with words like 'at one time', 'want' and so on.) From thus obeying the request to say 'red' to *applying* the word 'red' there is a significant jump; for whenever the child later uses the word it is not to be taken as obeying his original teacher, but as using part of his own language. This jump marks the transition from the *sound* 'red' to the *word* 'red'.

(10) The words used as examples here differ from each other. The child knows the domain of application of the signs 'red', 'green', 'hard', 'warm' (except for doubtful cases), after it has learnt to concentrate its attention on recognizing what is similar and calling it by the same name; when it has learnt to ignore possible differences in shade, position, time and so on. Not so with the sign 'before': even when it has learnt to use this sign between green and red in any positions and with varying intervals (corresponding, roughly, to various shades covered by the sign 'red'), the domain of use is not yet exhausted by far. The sign 'before' between two *definite* colours (or between two other sensory qualities) corresponds to the sign 'red'. But the former has a much wider domain of application (its omission would be more noticeable), for besides this analogous domain it comprises many others (quite apart from the fact that it is used for time and space and other kinds of orders). Therefore we say that the word 'before' is more complex. Besides it belongs to a different part of speech, which includes a substitution bar, namely: the sign 'before' can never be put in place of the sign 'red' (see 3). The word 'and' is even more complex; for in addition to the meaning that is analogous to 'before' (simultaneity), one has to become acquainted with it as a conjunction of sentences. In that sense it too belongs to a different part of speech.

2. ON DEFINITION

(1) We meet definitions in various forms: as assertions: 'people use the word *x* in the sense...'; as command: 'This word *should* be used in this way' or 'use the word thus'; as wish: 'Let this word be used thus', and so on. It belongs to the grammar of the last two cases that they occur only in future form, whereas definition as assertion refers to the past.

(2) Sometimes definition is treated as though it were a sentence that could be true or false. The similarity between definition and assertion misleads us into overlooking this grammatically important difference between them.

(3) A closer look shows however that definition *only seems* to occur as assertion: we must never forget the difference, lest we be tempted to confuse the two types of sentence.

(4) When a lawyer determines what constitutes theft or crime, he may wish to free concepts from arbitrary oscillation, or to describe the real boundaries, or to give new meaning to the material. In case one and three he *creates* language, in case two he *describes* it. Definition in the strict sense requires only the laying down of a norm; description is definition only insofar as the aim is at the same time to *obey* the described usage, or teach another to do so.

(5) Let us clarify the difference through examples: (a) 'tree means such and such' (followed by pointing or indications for the purpose of defining). This is not the same as (b) 'by tree, members of this or that linguistic region understand such and such'. For this last refers only to what has already happened, and if it refers to the future as well, it can be only a hypothesis that may be true or false; whereas the first sentence amounts to a decision, from which we deduce *the right* to use the word with this or that meaning.

(6) In checking whether a word is applicable in a given case, whether we should call *x* a tree, we do indeed call on usage as a touchstone: but this is not just comparison with usage; one who tries to remember whether some similar object was called a tree, is not a mere observer, for he has given *prior* assent to what is laid down in this language. If in doubt whether this is a tree or not, a man who is not a linguist (for in that case he often merely observes) usually regards himself as testing the object because he adheres to a linguistic community, as comparing the object with the community's usual rules and definitions of concepts so that he might use the word accordingly. If he finds that *x* is not a tree, this is in the first instance the result of comparison with usage (that is remembering situations in which one does or does not use the word); but his rejection too is based on his resolution to adhere to the statutes of the linguistic community, and this is important. If there is no decision, it is as when a judge cannot decide a difficult case.

(7) When a judge gives his decision, the latter cannot be translated as follows: 'for this action it has till now been customary to impose such and such punishment' or 'the legal code states that for this action the culprit shall be punished thus'. These would be historical statements that do not

lead to sentence being carried out; for from such statements it does not follow that the guilty man must go to prison. The same holds in language: many sentences referring to language are normative, like a judge's decisions.

(8) Before a judge gives his decision, he usually compares the case with various mutually correcting legal provisions (except in a very simple case in which the case falls clearly under a single heading). Likewise with a decision concerning the meaning of a concept. One compares the object (or concept, if it is a case of membership of a concept of higher order and the like) with the various acquired criteria and assimilated dispositions; often one needs to call on many criteria. With the word 'red' it is enough to sense the similarity in seeing. With the word 'man', the corrections are carried through automatically. But in some cases we become positively aware of this mutual correction based on various criteria.

(9) There are no undefinable concepts: if something is undefinable then it is not a concept. (A concept can be undefinable within a certain system of signs, but not *absolutely*.) It is too narrow a view of the concept of definition that has led to the notion of undefinable concepts. But since definition signifies any ranging of a sign within a linguistic system or any action that smoothes the path of understanding, whether by pointing, combinations of words, appeals to memory, samples and so on, there simply are no undefinable concepts: 'undefinable concept' is logically inadmissible. One may know of an object that it is a sign in language without being acquainted with its meaning: for such a person, this is then an *undefined* concept; but only those objects are *undefinable* that are not used in language. Thinking that there was a limit to definition, people racked their brains as to what lay beyond that limit; but language has no limit.

(10) There is a kind of definition that amounts to translation within the one language. Instead of a sign A one puts a combination of signs: B, C, D. For example: 'a piebald is a horse with white and black patches'. Many regard this kind of example as definition par excellence. This prejudice has given rise to many errors. Note that such definitions can be used only in certain cases; above all they cannot be used in cases where somebody does not know the signs B, C, D either, and in languages in which one and the same thing cannot be expressed in different ways.

(11) A definition is a rule that refers to linguistic usage. For this purpose let us examine the sentence: 'if you see something like this, say red'. This sentence can be an instruction on how to use the word: it enriches a person's language by the word 'red'. Analyzing the sentence, we find that 'something like this' signifies the paradigm, while 'say' means not pronounce but *call*. Our language acquires the word 'red' only *after* the sentence. It is not a command that bids us say 'red' whenever for example we see a red lamp, rather it orders us to use this material whenever we have occasion to *talk about* such lamps. The sentence may of course mean also an order in use; in which case 'something like this' means the full word or concept, 'say' means pronounce and 'red' the sound rather than the material of the *sign*. After that sentence our language is not enriched, for it presupposes a complete dictionary. To make this more plausible think of the engine driver to whom a red signal means 'stop'. This 'means' is of the second kind (an order in use, not a laying down of the meaning of 'stop.'

(12) The word 'eagle' means a flying eagle and this means heroism. Here one might think that the first meaning had in its turn a meaning. Let us show that this is not so: if the written sign 'eagle' (that is, the material) means an eagle and also heroism, this is simply a case of ambiguity. If then a flying eagle means heroism, *he* is the material of the sign heroism; as sign, however, as material *and* meaning it has no further meaning. What is meaning in one instance, may become material in another: one can use a table to express the word 'courageous'; at the same time the object table is the bearer of the meaning of the combination of letters TABLE. But material and meaning together cannot become further material. Thus the sign 'death's-head' is used for 'dead head' or for the picture of a death's-head (that is for the 'cross-section', see 3, or for the visible picture only). Moreover, the picture of a death's-head means poison. But only the *picture* means poison: you can draw a death's-head on a bottle or write 'poison' on it (both are fragmentary sentences). The bearer of a meaning may at the same time be the material of another meaning, but the material *and* the meaning together cannot be the material of a meaning of a higher rank.

(13) Definition by example: if someone asks me what is a glass, and I answer his question by pointing to one standing on the table, this pointing signifies a definition by paradigm. (One cannot show all the

objects that belong to the extension of a concept, because its application is to be unbounded in space and time, hence one chooses a paradigm.) Likewise if I am asked for the meaning of the sign '2' or 'mental process' and so on, and I answer by telling my interlocutor: 'You and I make two people' with the accent on 2; or 'Joy, grief and so on, these are mental processes'. Let us examine these three cases a little further. (i) Behind the seemingly very simple explanation of the sign 'glass' there is a whole series of explanations that are as it were presupposed. It is as when someone sees a mountain from afar, with declivities and winding paths unrevealed; for sometimes a word is used only to denote one point within *one* system; at other times it may denote the cross-section or selection of points of many systems. Shape, transparency, purpose, size, all together including zones of vagueness, is what we call a glass, and all this is 'meant' when I say 'this thing there is a glass'. But in explaining a 'simple sign' like 'red', too, we must presuppose (besides applicability to a range and without limit) that the hearer understands that the sign refers to the colour and not the size, shape or whatever else of the object (this forms part of the common disposition at the base of all communication). This is not an explicit assumption about the other person's mental processes but an automatic attunement that we take for granted. (ii) The example concerning the number 2 is much more complicated; for the domain of application of numbers includes things, feelings, meanings and so on, all of which is to be explained by paradigm. This makes much greater demands on our understanding, for I expect the hearer to apply this system 'multidimensionally'. (iii) In explaining the concept 'mental process' by enumerating some of these or by mentioning one, we presuppose beyond the dispositions mentioned in (i) two other abilities: that of letting *one* sign stand for different modes of behaviour (and of forming the cross-section of mood and conduct); and that of subsuming, or forming genera and species. Here one must thus proceed somewhat further before reaching what we may call 'simple signs'.

(14) To illustrate the machinery of language in this regard, consider an example: a tourist club, concerned about the welfare of hikers, has introduced a series of markings. To encourage the tired, the first colour code sign along the path is accompanied by the number 20, which here means that there are 20 more trees marked in this code before the destination. The following trees are marked from 19 to 1, the last one, at the

end, carries 0. This last corresponds to the pointing in the explanation of the sign 'red'. The explanation of the concept 'mental process' by means of 'joy' must be compared with one of the other markings which indicate that several more points must be passed before the goal.

(15) We said that a concept's rules of use constitute its meaning. Stating these rules is itself a kind of definition. An 'enumeration' too can be a useful definition, and so can stating the systems that intervene in the formation of a concept (that is, the definitions of 'content' in traditional logic).

(16) One often distinguishes between two kinds of definition: (i) an ostensive definition, or gesture (ii) a definition through linguistic signs (although pointing can occur by means of language alone, without gesture, for example by means of the command: 'Go left round the corner and look at the wall there, it is red'). Which method is preferred is a matter of convenience. For example one will hardly try to explain the words 'virtuous' and 'courageous' (abbreviations for modes of behaviour) by performance of virtuous and courageous acts, but rather by giving sentences in which the words are applied according to usage and others in which they are not, and the like. That seems to be at the root of the grammatical difference between 'concrete' and 'abstract'. Signs are called concrete if the first method is technically more convenient, and abstract if the second method is preferred.

(17) Some concepts are explained by indicating the meaning of their negation; for example rest in terms of motion, good in terms of bad and so on. All these are methods and ways of definition.

(18) The well-known vetoes relating to mistakes in defining are at first no more than advice and signposts towards better and more correct definition. They are not logical rules of language; they are often not obeyed, without this causing contravention of logical rules. Only 'circular' definition must be rejected, because it fails to satisfy the definition of definition (that is, the ranging of the sign into the fabric of language).

3. PARTS OF SPEECH AND SUBSTITUTION

(1) The words of a language may be grouped from various points of view. We are mainly interested in an arrangement according to possibilities of substitution. Words that belong to the same kind may be

substituted for each other without depriving the sentence of sense. Apart from this classification which contains a substitution licence, others, too, are logically important, because assembling like and excluding unlike. An example of the first more complete mode of classification into parts of speech are colours and numbers: the corresponding words are ideally substitutable: in place of 'green' one can sensibly put 'red' but not 'three'; in place of 'four', 'two' but not 'yellow'. An example of the second mode are proper names and general names: 'virtue' and 'table' are general names and thereby different from 'John' and 'Rome'. But one cannot substitute 'virtue' for 'table': this would turn many sentences into nonsense, although the two share the grammar of general names.

(2) The concepts of language are not to be grouped according to *one* schema. Our language with the systems that are united in it resembles a geographical chart on which are marked meridians and latitudes, mountain ranges, customs, weather and the like, by means of various colours, shadings, and lines. For example height may be rendered by colour, vegetation by lines, temperature by spots of various size and so on. Each of these systems of signs is independent and justified from a certain point of view. Two signs of one and the same system can be substituted for each other, but neither can be put in place of a sign belonging to a different system.

(3) From the wealth of classifications let us take some examples: (a) the traditional doctrine of categories points to parts of speech. The category of whole and parts relates to general names, the category of identity and difference to comparative words, the category of action to active verbs and so on. (The category of substance relates to the pecularity of our language that makes a certain concept the bearer of the sentence. See II, 6 ,'Subject and Substantive'. Substantives are 'the pillars of the sentence', 'permanent', not amenable to comparison, and invariant to the flow of time, that is to conjugation.) (b) A classification suggested by modern ways of thought: (i) Names for elements from the domain of a single sense (sight, touch and so on): 'red', 'blue', 'hard' and so on. These are closed systems consisting of two or more members. Within each member one can introduce a further system of three or more members, as we shall see; for example 'warm' and 'cold', and for each of these two the usual comparisons 'warm', 'warmer', 'warmest', 'cold', 'colder', 'coldest'. (ii) Words given by different domains of sense and

other systems, such as: 'water', 'table', 'milk', 'tree'. Analysis reveals something that looks so and so, is found here and there and used for such and such a purpose and much else, in which some determinations are relevant and others more or less irrelevant. It is a selection of elements from different systems. (We are using amongst other things systems of the first group, for example 'white' – 'black', 'hard' – 'soft'.) This type of word will be called a cross-section of the systems. (To see how schemata, intersect, we note that 'to write' and 'tree' belong to the second group, but the one is an activity and the other a thing. From that point of view they belong to different parts of speech.) Vagueness in cross-sections consists in one's not knowing which systems must be involved and which are irrelevant; vagueness in the prior concepts relates merely to the lack of a metric within the system concerned (see II, 9). (iii) Place, time and value systems and so on, such as: 'left' – 'right', 'earlier' – 'later', 'top' – 'bottom', 'good' – 'bad' and the like. Each member of such a system can itself become a system (as with 'warm' in (i)). These systems differ widely from one another. The members of each individual system can be replaced by each other. (iv) Terms for systems of different kind (that is for systems of signs and operations, See Part One, III, 5) for example colour, thing, number, space, time. (The signs for systems spring from the desire for clarity. They further enable one to speak about collections without considering the details. Systems 'in themselves' are words in language.) (v) Collections of modes of behaviour, such as 'mourning', 'life' and so on. This classification may be further developed. (The traditional classification into parts of speech at the root of Chapter II belongs here, too.)

(4) We further mention the group of languages in which the logic of parts of speech stands out with peculiar prominence, namely African class languages, in which a word's belonging to a part of speech is explicitly marked.

(5) In many ways, language may be compared with a machine composed of many disparate parts. To classify the parts, one may proceed in various ways, depending on what mark or marks are chosen as principle of classification. We distinguish between two kinds of grouping: one more, the other less strict. In the former, each member can replace any other member of the same group. The latter are groups whose members sometimes stand for one another, sometimes not: they belong to the

same group only insofar as they can replace each other. The strict case is subject also to the veto of using two signs of the same system at once: 'This spot is green and red at once' is barred; 'green and cold' however is admissible (for two signs of different systems can be used at once). 'Earlier' cannot at the same time be 'later', nor 'East' 'West' or 'up' 'down' and so on (this follows from using the rule of contradiction in forming these systems). To take the simile of the machine: here are two parts that may change places and do for each other, but not two in *one* place. This rule does not apply to the less strict groups: their members cannot always replace each other, but two may appear at the same time. Here too there may be substitutions, for example 'the tiger is standing on the right' and 'the table is standing on the right'. Insofar as many sentences remain significant if 'tiger' is replaced by 'table' (if what matters is merely occupation by a visible or touchable space filler), both belong to the same part of speech. But insofar as one can say 'the tiger claws an animal', yet not 'the table claws an animal' without feeling upset by this offence against linguistic rules, the two concepts belong to different parts of speech. (Here one must always distinguish between the *empirical fact* that tables show no signs of life and the *grammatical rule* based on this fact: once the rule is introduced, the sentence 'a table claws an animal' is no longer false, but against the rules. If we compare our grammar with that of an animistic tribe, it may turn out that expressions like 'killing the stone' forbidden to us are admissible in their grammar.)

(6) Any principle of classification that aims at absolute rule must be regarded from the outset as a reform of language. If one wants to describe the actually prevailing conditions, one must reckon with a multiplicity of overlapping systems.

4. ONE MEANING, OR MANY?

(1) Grammatical explanation often moves between the two poles of *one* as against *many* meanings. If someone wants to give the word 'is' a single meaning only, we must show him sentences like 'twice two is four', 'man is an animal', 'the tower here is at the back', to point to the different meanings. But if he wants to give two meanings to the word 'walking' in 'two men are walking on the road' according to whether the sentence occurs in a fairy tale or in an ordinary report, then we ask him whether

the same applies to the word 'two' or 'on' and the like, in order to convert him to the *one* meaning. In sentences that have different 'keys', the words nevertheless retain the same meaning. The word 'give' in the command 'give me a glass of water!' and in the assertion 'A has given B a glass of water' means the same; and likewise all the other words. Otherwise we should need a different dictionary for every type of sentence. Part of the convention as to meaning is that it remains invariant towards *types* of sentence. We read the sentence 'two men are walking on the road' in a fairy tale and in a historical report. Not only the words 'two' and 'men' obey the same 'accidence', but also 'walk', although in general it is immaterial in the fairy tale where and when they walked; likewise 'road', though it generally makes no odds which road. Only the syntax of combination of sentences differentiates the fairy tale from the historical report.

(2) Figuratively speaking, every language has its 'vocabulary', in which some words have indices, so that 'is', for English, appears as 'is$_1$', 'is$_2$' and so on. (See III, 13.) Likewise, metaphors carry special indices. But the use of words in commands, laws of nature, anecdotes and so on, is not marked by indices.

(3) However, it is often difficult to distinguish precisely between words with indices and those that have *one* meaning.

(4) It is misleading, too, always to confine words to special areas of application, for language seeks to overcome the particular and to exalt the intersection of meanings as *the* meaning.

(5) One might express it thus: if in a certain linguistic community (that is, where certain motives have produced a certain marked linguistic form) a word such as 'good', 'beautiful' and so on occurs without being felt as ambiguous (that is, one who grew up in the language, perhaps trained by comparison with other languages and proper study of grammar, so that his sense of language is adequately schooled, does not feel any difference); then we say that the word is the cross-section of the meanings, and we may properly ask for the common part of its grammar: 'what is good?', 'what is beautiful?' are in this sense legitimate questions. It may of course happen that in answering such single questions that the words are indeed ambiguous so that the meanings have no intersection. In that case our current feeling for language was misleading; for it is a big mistake to overlook the throwing together of many disparate meanings; and likewise, to overlook what is common to meanings.

5. EXAMPLES OF LOGICAL VETOES

(1) Word combinations such as 'green virtue', 'square virtue' are barred from a vocabulary (senseless, for 'vetoed' in this context is identical with 'senseless'), because a combination of sentences formed with them will on analysis yield senseless sentences: 'the green virtue of John may be traced back to the event Y'; analysis gives 'John is virtuous', 'virtue is green', 'Y has occurred', 'John's virtue is caused by Y'. Amongst these is the sentence 'virtue is green', which is senseless, and therefore a corresding combination of concepts is barred from the dictionary.

(2) This is usually decided by a predicative sentence marked in English by the copula 'is', which, amongst other things, serves to express the correspondence of two points chosen from different systems (See Part Two, III, 13). This type of sentence shows whether the two systems can occur together: if the constituent is translated into a sentence and the predication is unexceptionable, the word combination is permissible; if not, the sentence is senseless, and with it the word combination.

(3) Let us illustrate this on the quoted example: 'virtue is green' or 'square'. Virtue represents modes of behaviour in *substantive* form, comprising many kinds of human conduct: those adduced as paradigms are certain activities (or omissions) that we call 'valued actions' (that is activities combined with the two term system 'good' – 'evil'). But to none of these correspond colours or shapes. Sentences like 'X walks greenly' are barred. Likewise, those valued actions that come under 'virtue' are without colour or shape. Hence the sentence 'virtue is green' is against the rules. (The motive leading to these vetoes and the conventions that have been laid down about them are so basic that modes of expression like 'walk greenly' count as symptoms for a disturbed state of mind. One can conceive motives that might cause such forms of language.)

(4) We therefore distinguish between barred concepts and barred sentences. A concept is barred if it consists of incompatible parts, that is parts that translate into a nonsensical sentence; usually a predicative sentence that exhibits the incompatibility. Concepts like 'four-cornered triangle' or 'one day week' must be taken out of the sentence and turned separately into predications: 'this or that triangle is fourcornered', 'this or that week has one day' and so on. Since these are senseless because contradictory (because in forming these systems we have intro-

duced substitution rules that presuppose the rule of contradiction), we call the concepts contradictory. (As an example of a *general* predication we may take the expression 'mortal man', to be translated into 'all men are mortal'. An analogous barred expression is 'or-man' = 'all men are or'.)

(5) If I say 'the square is triangular', 'a man of thirty is younger than one of twenty', these sentences are barred as much as saying 'it is raining and not raining', though this last fails as a *combination of sentences* whereas the former fail on their own from the start.

(6) The colour system forbids predications within the one field, such as 'blue is red', just as the number system forbids '20 = 30'. The veto on 'blue is red' rests on the grammar of the colour system, which in turn presupposes the rule of contradiction. To predicate elements of certain systems of each other there is a rule that requires a bearer: there must be an object or point in space or time and the like, that is to serve as *intersection*. Without such intermediary the systems must by convention remain unconnected. Sentences like 'blue is cold', 'good is tall' without bearers are barred; but 'the blue object is cold', 'the good man is tall' are allowed. To distinguish between the two vetoes (that for predication within and that between systems), assign the elements to a bearer: for the first veto the sentence remains senseless ('the blue object is red' is barred as much as 'blue is red'); the second veto does not apply here.

(7) If concepts are often used correctly, offending against established conventions that are regarded as obvious will provoke our protest. With many combinations of concepts, however, one needs some reflection to 'discover' the offence. Take for example (i) 'Yesterday you will walk'. 'I am my father's father'. It is true and false (sweet and sour, white and red) at once. (In the last case 'at once' needs to be made more precise to provoke the 'inhibition'.) (ii) 'I feel your pain'. 'I can know what is false'. 'A exists but no one can ascertain it'. 'It is good in itself'. 'It would be better for me had I never been born'; and many others.

6. THE SO-CALLED HIGHEST LAWS OF LOGIC

(a)   The law of identity $A = A$.

(b)   The law of contradiction.

(c)   The law of excluded middle (tertium non datur).

(1) To begin with we note that the laws of logic are rules or grammatical observations; the former insofar as they are general prescriptions, the latter insofar as they describe situations found in language.

(2) (a) differs from (b) and (c) firstly in that it holds for *all* languages. Wherever signs are introduced, the convention holds that we designate not only the here and now, nor nominate as bearer of a sign only the material to hand at the moment; rather, it must be valid to use other similar materials for similar things. That is the most general prerequisite without which no understanding and no language is possible. The law of identity $(A=A)$ expresses the convention that changes of space and time (and often even of shape and the like) should not entail changes in name; moreover, it signifies 'these two similar signs that otherwise differ (as to space and so on) are to be equated as linguistic signs'.

(3) In contrast with (a), (b) and (c) relate to negation or the difference between true and false. However, we can imagine a language in which no negation occurs: it might for example consist only of wishes or commands, but no rejections. In such a language there would be no affirmation either; for, grammatically, negation belongs to affirmation. Nor would there be true or false, for these presuppose negation. (What is meant is not the *sign* but the *function* of negation within the language; for as to the sign, we can imagine three types: (i) a language that marks both affirmative and negative sentences with a certain sign, (ii) only negative sentences are marked by a special sign, as in most known languages; for example: 'here lies a book', not 'here lies yes a book', but 'here lies *no* book', (iii) only positive sentences are marked, let us say by 'yes'.) Such a language would have very slight grammatical multiplicity (slight compared with that of our own; for it would be indeed complete and ours too can be amplified). Rules (b) and (c) would be missing.

(4) However, taking away negation would perhaps impoverish language in the most radical way possible. A specialized and differentiated way of life demands assertions that can be denied and are true or false. We can thus understand why the laws of contradiction and excluded middle, which are simply the grammar of negation, (in connection with conjunction, disjunction and so on), are given so prominent a place.

(5) Nevertheless, we must avoid raising these laws to divine status and indulging in a logical cult. They are not the highest laws of thought or of the universe, nor do they inhabit some supernatural sphere: they aɹ

the grammar of those signs and operations that have great significance and occur in all known languages. In our way of putting it, one might say that they are a grammatical system for which there is the strongest of motives.

(6) Rules (b) and (c) can be expressed as grammatical commands. (b) would become: do not conjoin a sentence with its negation. Do not affirm or deny (the same thing) at once; do not say that something is true and false at once. (c) would become: use the words 'yes' and 'no', 'true' and 'false' (or 'obeyed' and 'not obeyed' in the case of commands) in such a way that if an asserted sentence is true, the corresponding denied one be false. (Both might however be expressed as grammatical observations.)

(7) (c) states that we may not assume a value between truth and falsehood, the way $\frac{1}{2}$ lies between 1 and 0.

(8) (c) presupposes (b). In (c) we observe that the system T–F (or that of affirmation–negation) is a closed system without further elements.

(9) As to (b) and (c), we note finally that they apply to themselves. One cannot say: 'Do not conjoin a sentence with its negation and do conjoin them'. (Likewise for the formulation of (b) as an observation, for (b) holds for assertions and commands.) Likewise for (c).

7. ONE LOGIC OR MANY?

(1) The answer to this question depends on what one understands by logic: if it is the examination of signs, meaning, rules and so on, there is only one logic – reflection on the nature of signs and rules as such belongs to *the* logic of all types of language; if it is observations about nouns, numbers, negation and various other systems, there are as many logics as types of language and linguistic systems.

(2) Suppose wars were to cease altogether and men no longer had any reasons for using weapons: then a part of language would disappear and become a topic for scholars. If poverty were to disappear, our language would lose the corresponding words and rules. Would this alter the logic of language? General logical reflection would remain the same, but the list of rules would be smaller by some rules.

(3) These examples concern small changes in life and language. One may however imagine much greater changes that could turn the whole

formation of concepts upside down. The changes in language would then be correspondingly greater and the treatise on logic more different. Even the law of contradiction might be absent, if the motive for forming negative sentences were lacking. *But the general veto that signs cannot be arbitrarily substituted for one another, and the rule that excludes the singularity of signs, are common to all languages.*

8. ABOUT THE SO-CALLED PERFECT LANGUAGE

(1) A language can become more perfect if its concepts are more precise and its sentence types more sharply distinct.

(2) One can cope with the vagueness of concepts in various ways, depending on what group of concepts is concerned: (i) with signs belonging to 'vague' systems, by introducing a precise metric in each (for example 'large'=anything over 30 ft), that is abolishing the systems' elasticity and imprecision. (ii) with signs previously called cross-sections, by laying down what systems are necessary and sufficient for a concept; for example, that 'table' should be determined by size, colour, number of feet and everything else like purpose, shape and so on is to be excluded. All this can be asked and implemented for the sake of precision. Similarly for other types of words.

(3) In the same way one can for instance bar sentences that oscillate between definition and assertion, or those that look now like commands and now like wishes; or else give them an external mark to banish the danger of confusion.

(4) So long as we speak of more or less perfect languages, we are moving within a legitimate field. Not so if we consider the possibility of an absolutely perfect language, for in this discussion the concept 'perfect language' offends against grammar.

(5) To explain this, let us try to describe some concepts of such a perfect language. For lamp we have sign A; for house, B. For the definition of 'house' and 'lamp' let there be a purely metric system. Thus a house is 30 ft high, broad and wide, a lamp only 4 cubic inches, all other systems being excluded. But even this language could not be perfect; for if I use A once more, we must make a convention about the sign's material. For example, A must have the same meaning whether it be written in ink, pencil and so on. Moreover, we should have to indicate

the minimum size of A, whether microscopes are admissible and so on. In using the metric system we must indicate under what circumstances one says a thing is 30 ft high, which requires sight and touch and its attendant conditions, and this last will involve vaguenesses that can be removed only in part by precise stipulations. Indeed, this discourse in principle contains all the vaguenesses of language. Were one to try to do without them, one could not speak of 30 ft or of A. The language would as it were cancel itself: an absolutely perfect language is no language.

9. TRUTH

(1) The question of verifying a sentence can be answered only *after* it has been ranged as to grammar. If it is a combination of sentences, one must first find the key for proceeding in this connection. For one must lay down whether one is dealing with assertions concerning individual events, laws of nature, anecdotes and so on.

(2) The single sentences must be examined to see whether they are assertions, commands, wishes and so on. For only assertions can be true or false. If it has already been established that one is dealing with an assertion, various other matters must be considered before the question as to truth can be put unambiguously.

(3) Take the assertion: 'Yesterday there was a wolf here'. The grammatical ranging of the sentence depends on whether this is to convey that the wolf was seen (a) by myself only, (b) by others as well or (c) by others only. These determine what is meant by observing 'that is true'. If (a), the sentence is true so soon as there is a memory of the fact, so that I have no further doubts; for that is precisely what the sentence expresses. If (c), the sentence is true only when I know that those who assert it are not dreamers, liars and so on, nor are others who may in some way confirm the sentence, and the like. The conditions the sentence fulfils when we say it is true are different from those under (a). As to (b) it is a mixture of (a) and (c) which in a certain sense correct each other.

(4) A picture or photograph too can, if desired, be called true, insofar as it is a faithful reproduction; and if not, false. Truth then means adequacy of the picture. But this would be a metaphorical sense of the word 'true'; here it would mean similarity of the individual parts, but mostly that of the total expression, with what is represented. Since the picture is

no linguistic expression, it cannot be true in the ordinary sense, as is shown also by the fact that one cannot negate a picture.

(5) In a sentence the individual parts do not resemble the concept represented, except in a hieroglyphic script. But even in a pictorial script we already have a language insofar as the pictures become signs. Even the most faithful representation of a house is no sign, so long as no convention has been made about it. (In pictographic script a pattern is chosen as sign, which often saves one the trouble of explanation by paradigm.) One who compares language with a picture, and regards truth as adequacy of the picture, must remember that this is a remote simile.

(6) One might compare language with a construction kit: it contains various materials and some instructions for using them. Although this image is preferable to that of the picture insofar as it can explain the multiple use of the same material, it is still too simple to clarify all aspects of language. (For example one can hardly use it to illustrate negation: that requires other models.)

(7) One cannot ask after the truth of a question, command or logical rule; for a question is a request and not an assertion, and likewise a command and a logical rule. Only a sentence concerning the fact, that there has been a question, command or laying down of a logical rule, can be true or false.

(8) One sometimes speaks of truth within a certain context, for example that in Shakespeare it is true that Romeo loved Juliet. This, in a sense, is correct, namely insofar as that is what is stated in the play, even if it may be historically false. But this is not to be explained in terms of a separate concept of poetic truth as against historic truth. Truth and falsehood relate to assertions and these can be only true or false. However, fiction has a special 'key' imposing translation prior to verification (see Part Two, IV, 7).

(9) 'Truth of a natural law' means, that the law has till now proved true, so that we expect it to go on doing so. Since natural laws hold for the future without indication until when, they will be regarded as true so long as they have not been found wanting.

(10) If someone interprets the word 'true' in the sense of 'useful' or 'interesting to me (or to us)', as pragmatism does, he confuses the motive for introducing a concept with the *meaning* of the concept; for very

likely we came to formulate the difference between 'true' and 'false' through wishing to differentiate the useful from the harmful. But that is not the meaning or usage of the signs 'true' and 'false'.

(11) 'True' in the sense of 'genuine' relates to concepts (general names) and means: very close (similar) to the paradigm adduced for explaining the concept. For example, true nonsense, the whale is not a true fish. Here, too, we have a different meaning of the word.

(12) If one asks after the truth of a historical event, one is usually referred to documents, that is the statements of others who have seen something. Moreover, one is referred to a plausible chain of events, that is the course of past events is compared with the otherwise known course. Moreover, one compares the mode of representation of an historical report with that of accounts by our own contemporaries, to infer as to reliability and the like. Nevertheless, that the statements are true is a surmise that may be more or less probable. Often reports correct one another as to accuracy, details and so on. After these corrections that depend on our technical equipment, a sentence will be declared true, that is regarded as true so long as nothing speaks against it. The truth of historical reports in this respect resembles the truth of natural laws. But they differ in that historical reports can at best become highly improbable in the light of other reports, whereas a natural law becomes *false* in the light of contrary experience.

10. CONCEPT AND SENTENCE, SENSE AND MEANING

(1) In our language, isolated concepts occur only in dictionaries or in grammar or in discussions about these; otherwise, only as constituents of sentences. Concepts exist so to speak only *before* use.

(2) Indeed, man is not primarily an arranger of concepts, nor his language a card index.

(3) We sometimes say 'this linguistic structure lies between concept and sentence'. This can mean only that it is sometimes the one and sometimes the other, since both at once is logically impossible. For example, the word 'God' may occur as concept or as fragment of the sentence 'God help us!' and so on (but it may be simply a way of reacting, that is neither concept nor sentence; this holds from the point of view both of the exclaimer and of the hearer who can interpret it only as symptom) ·

For general language, however, it is either a sentence or a concept, according to the presence or absence of the exclamation mark in writing. Similarly for the spoken word: according to the situation.

(4) The greeting 'good morning' is usually not a sentence, since nothing is intended by it. In certain cases these words carry no meaning, for if this were to be taken as a sentence expressing a wish, the speaker who when asked whether he had wished the other a good morning replied 'no, I never thought of it' would have to be called a liar, which is obviously not so; for there is a convention that in certain cases these words be neither concept nor sentence.

(5) In some commands the material looks as though it was concepts: 'come!' 'speak!' and the like. But they are sentences.

(6) One could imagine a language in which sentences consisted in single syllables, with certain syllables corresponding to certain situations, for example 'the dog is barking'=ti. Such a language would have no separate signs for things, sensations and so on. One might compare it with an old weapon that can only be used in some definite manner but not dismantled. It requires immense experience to pursue the craft of language, isolating concepts and always reassembling them afresh.

(7) Languages do not consider the temporal sequence of observation. If I say 'John is walking' it is not a case of my first observing the presence of a man and then his walking. My representation follows linguistic usage and not the sequence of observation. (In cases where it matters to indicate the earlier and later, one sometimes finds poetic clichés like 'John, he walks, how tall he is' and so forth. The structure of such accounts differs from the rest of language. If the whole language followed this pattern, and one always followed the sequence of experience, a sentence like 'John is walking' could not occur at all, no matter what was experienced first. In such a language this sentence would indeed be senseless.)

(8) The relation of thought to sentence is this: a thought is a sentence not perceivable by the senses. To an indefinite thought (feeling) there corresponds an indefinite sentence, such as 'someone who somehow interests us was lately in our surroundings' and the like.

(9) A sentence may often be verified in various ways: by one's own observation, statements of others, comparison between statements and so on. The sense of the sentence is the essence of many methods of verifica-

tion (just as a concept is often the essence of many 'locations'); hence we say it is the 'same sentence' whose truth is ascertained by various methods. (The possibility of translating a sentence within the same language without changing it, depends on the wealth of the language which enables us to express one situation in several ways. Here, too, we say that it is the same sentence; by which we mean that using different materials does not affect the sense of the sentence.)

(10) The *meaning* of a word is the content of the conventions laid down about this word; its position in grammar and in the vocabulary of the language; the point of purchase of the rules that apply; what we understand by it and the like. Just so, the *sense* of a sentence is what is intended by the sentence; its place in the fabric of language; the mode of its use; the essence of all methods of verification and so on. All these ways may be followed to make the grammatical concepts 'sense' and 'meaning' more familiar. These ways differ as to usefulness in proportion as they serve to give us correct insight, but they must not be misused nor turned into occult qualities.

(11) The meaning of words and the sense of sentences follow the 'average usage', that is, frequent mode of use. If A says to B 'give me an apple' and he meant merely something edible, and B understood him (that is, gathered from the situation that he might equally well supply a pear), then 'an apple' to them means simply 'something edible'. The command was obeyed by B giving A an edible object, but this holds only for A and B for whom in this instance the sign 'apple' has a special meaning. Another person (or even A and B in different circumstances) uses 'apple' with a different meaning, and we are justified in saying that B did not obey A's command.

11. FRAGMENTARY SENTENCES

(1) If someone enters a coffee bar and says 'one white' this is a fragmentary sentence left to the hearer to complete. Whenever a regular sentence is heard or read, there is a surmise, namely that the speaker or writer uses the words with a definite meaning. In the case of fragmentary sentences there is the further surmise that certain words should be added.

(2) Logically, the above words are identical with 'give me a cup of coffee with lots of milk'. Only because both phrases occur in our lan-

guage do we call the former a 'fragmentary sentence': because a longer sentence (that is, one containing more concepts than are generally used) corresponds to the fragment, although both are the same as to sense. Since the words 'give me' have other uses and their own meanings, we speak of a fragmentary sentence where they are missing.

(3) Imagine the following situation: we are reading a book in which some parts are blotted out with strips of paper. However, the obscured words can be inferred from the context. Alongside the regular 'automatic' surmise that occurs whenever we read a book, we must moreover discover the missing words from the context of the sentence. In this case, if we are restricted to this one exemplar, the sentences that are partly illegible are fragmentary.

(4) However, it often happens in the reading of papyri that because the document is severely damaged, the reader cannot speak of fragmentary sentences at all. We then have an aggregate of words that can be ascertained, but do not form a sentence. Here we can at best surmise, that it was a sentence or that it will turn out to be one. For the present reader, however it is not a fragmentary sentence. For a fragment exists only where some signs are missing yet the sentence as a whole remains.

(5) 'Aha', (now I understand) is a complete sentence, and even has a 'key'. For it can concern only an assertion about understanding. Such one-word sentences require no completion inasmuch as they belong to a type of speech in which situations can be rendered by single signs.

12. On stress

(1) The melody of the sentence, the stressing of single signs and pauses are often like written or spoken words. The rise and fall of tone can make the sentence a question or command and often mark the grammatical structure of the sentence.

(2) 'On Wédnesday Í am góing tó Lóndon'. This sentence can be stressed in five ways. The assessment of it as true or false here follows stress. For often certain parts of the sentence are irrelevant. For example, sometimes the day does not matter. Someone might say 'I am going on Wednesday', but in the event go on Thursday, without this counting as falsification if that is not the point; however, if the stress is on 'Wednesday', then the sentence has been falsified. Stress ensures that part of the

sentence is neglected in analysis. The stress on 'Wednesday' makes us aware that beside the sentence 'I am going to London' there is another that must be verified independently: 'I am going on Wednesday'. Likewise for the stress on the other words.

(3) The question 'Are you (i) going (ii) now (iii)?' can be examined as to the position of the main accent on i, ii or iii and the corresponding completion. The accent on ii may for example sometimes mean 'why not stay?'; that on i, according to the case, may have to be completed by 'why not he?' and the like. Similarly for iii. But stress may be excluded altogether in the interest of a general average, in which case one follows the general average meaning of a certain turn of phrase in the given linguistic habitat. However, stress itself is treated according to its linguistic average, with due regard to the given circumstances insofar as this seems necessary for understanding the stress as used in this linguistic setting. Only those who have known each other long enough interpret stress in a special way, in which case the 'average' relates to the behaviour of these persons.

(4) 'Are you coming today?' This can be stressed in three ways, each of which presupposes the general interrogative melody, expressed in writing by the question mark. This conveys (i) I am asking (ii) the question is to be analyzed in certain ways. Thus we distinguish the melody and the stress of the sentence, and the sense of a sentence differs according to changes in either. Stress has meaning, for if not, it would be irrelevant, as is volume. But the difference between soft and loud can be used as a sign too. The usual convention is that sense is volume invariant, but occasionally another convention can be laid down, traces of which are found in our language.

(5)   (a) *London* is the capital of Great Britain.
       (b) London is the capital of Great Britain.

In (a) we somehow already know the concepts used, we are moving within applied language and announce that in the series of capitals and towns as such these two points correspond with one another. But in (b) we may have a case of definition, in which a name is fixed, we are moving within the field of namegiving. The difference shows in stress.

(6) *The* horse, the *horse* are logically different. Indeed, the difference is one of the most important in logic, namely that between

proper names and general names, and here shows through stress.

13. METAPHOR

(1) The expressions 'dead words', 'living words', 'laughing sun' and the like are metaphors, that is combinations of signs that at first blush offend against the rules of language; but usage gave permission admitting them provided they are unobjectionably translated.

(2) Consider some examples of metaphor 'To find death': since death is not a perceivable object that can be appropriated, but a collection of differences in behaviour of living beings, one cannot *find* it; the expression here means 'to die'.

(3) 'To live in the memory of posterity (or, of descendants)': here 'to live' means no more than that others talk about the figure, actions, character of a man. One could say equally well 'to live in photographs, after death'.

(4) 'The tooth of time'. A word that denotes an ordering system, like 'time', has no teeth. One might think that a sentence containing this expression defies verification since the way is barred: however, the way lies through translation and analysis, which come under usage. ('The tooth of time' is translated, 'The tooth of space' not; if everybody used his own metaphors we should have a confusion of tongues as at the tower of Babel.)

(5) We distinguish between metaphorical concepts and metaphorical expressions. A word becomes metaphorical if a sign is constantly used outside its proper sphere of meaning, because of some often remote similarity. *One* characteristic is selected and for economy's sake the word is used in spite of disparity as to other characteristics. Metaphorical expressions like 'neck of a bottle' exhibits such similarity in the *collocation* of the concepts; as in 'to pull it out of one's hat'.

(6) In ordinary language the advice to translate before verifying (or before obeying a command and so on) is almost superfluous, since the sentences will be correctly understood anyway. All the more one must insist on translation in certain 'clever' discussions.

(7) Euphemism is a special case of metaphor, namely those that have as common ground a reluctance to use the usual material and the consequent convention to use something else.

(8) 'The camel is the ship of the desert'. To deal with metaphors of this sort, we must first translate the sentence into 'the camel serves the same end in deserts as ships on the sea'. More precisely: (i) 'ships serve to carry men or objects from one point of the sea to another (from shore to shore)'. (ii) 'The camel serves to carry men or objects from one point of the desert to another (from edge to edge)'. (iii) 'In this respect the camel resembles a ship'.

(9) If in a sentence 'ship of the desert' occurs in the sense of 'camel', there are three possibilities: (i) I do not know the metaphor and therefore say the combination of words is senseless, (ii) I know the metaphor and say that the sign is meant metaphorically thus containing the above mentioned three sentences. (The result of analysis of a sentence containing this expression must include those three sentences, apart from others.) (iii) 'ship of the desert' may be used as an established sign synonymous with 'camel' without asserting the three sentences, so that the result of analysis does not now include them.

14. HYPERBOLE

(1) 'One moment, please!' 'It took ages'. Idioms like these are to be translated into normal language according to the conventions and then to be verified. Hyperbole thus follows the rule of metaphor.

(2) 'It is dreadfully painful' is no hyperbole. Anyone who has experienced pain knows that the word 'very', worn out as it is through use, fails to express the right feeling. 'Dreadfully' here is a further step of comparison.

(3) 'Dear Sir' is according to convention equivalent to 'Sir'. Often the person addressed is not dear, so that on removing 'brackets' from the expression to be translated, no further sentence appears. For the phrase would be used only if the person spoken to were indeed dear, one would have to divide the expression into (i) 'Mr. X, please listen to me' (ii) 'Mr. X is dear'. But since it is a polite formula, only the first sentence is intended. Often such formulae mean nothing. Nor is it regarded as a contradiction, if the letter reveals the opposite. For here a special convention has been laid down.

15. DIALECT AND COMMON LANGUAGE

(1) As to the material used one distinguishes between dialect and

standard language. Likewise as to meaning too: certain meanings occurring here and there are excluded from the common language, for if all differences of meaning (for different people, places, times and so on) were taken into account, it becomes difficult to find one's way in language. Hence we exclude those meanings that have failed to establish themselves generally.

(2) By the usual word 'usage' one intends what is common to linguistic peculiarities of single individuals, classes, dialects and so on, within a more or less vaguely defined linguistic area, while doubtful cases as to material or meaning follow such usage as has prevailed or is accepted by experts.

(3) But if in a linguistic region a usage contrary to rules prevails (that is, people there speak in such a way that the rules that can be read off from what is spoken are disobeyed), we call this usage senseless. Such usage is observed by asking speakers directly or indirectly for the rules of their own language, so that in its own name we can then assert that this or that mode of expression is against the rules. This is to begin with an observed fact. But since most people feel the desire to speak in an orderly way and dislike acknowledging that their language is confused, we use the opportunity to hold them back from senseless combinations of words. This happens at times in philosophic discussions.

Here we distinguish various parts of a discussion: (i) the observation of the rules of general usage outside philosophy, by means of producing sentences that contain the words in question. (ii) The observation of what rules the person does in fact follow, by asking him. (iii) The observation of how (i) and (ii) differ, to maintain clarity. (iv) If the person fails to keep to his own rules, this fact is now observed. (v) An appeal to his desire for orderly speech. (i) – (iv) are observations, (v) is a demand based on commands he has accepted by agreeing to follow certain rules.

16. PUNCTUATION

(1) The comma has various functions. For instance (a) before a relative pronoun introducing an amplifying clause (but not a defining clause): 'The man, who...' (concept and amplifying clause analyse into two separate sentences). (b) between clauses of a complex sentence: 'If A, then B', to separate the parts (here premiss and conclusion). (c) in place of

'and', in which case the comma is to be taken as a logical constant:
'John, Harry and Peter are walking' = 'John is walking and Harry is
walking and Peter is walking'.

(2) The comma is the symbol of separation and connection simultaneously. It depends from which side one wants to look at it: from the
side of analysis or from that of synthesis.

(3) A comma before 'and' between nouns (but not between clauses)
is superfluous, as also before 'or', as the words by themselves indicate
the structure.

(4) The full stop, in contrast with the comma, marks separation only.
Nevertheless, a full stop differs from the end of a book, in that the
former leads one to expect some further elucidation of the context,
whereas the latter leaves no such expectation. Hence the end of a book
is often marked by the word 'end' or by some graphic ornament. A new
paragraph or chapter lie between the full stop and the conclusion of the
topic they correspond to longer pauses in speech. (These help understanding and reflection.)

(5) Semicolon and full stop often are indistinguishable. But if the
semicolon indicates compatibility (contrast and the like), then it is a
material that does not merely mark the end of the sentence.

(6) The colon before a quotation allows us to use the words of the person
quoted as though he was speaking them. It is thus an instruction for
translating. But it has other functions too; for example, introducing a
clause that gives a reason: 'it is too late to shut the stable door: the
horse has bolted'.

(7) Quotation marks sometimes fulfil the first mentioned function of
the colon, but sometimes they must be translated as a separate sentence,
such as 'I am not quite satisfied with this term' and the like.

(8) The exclamation mark often indicates commands, and interroga-
tion mark questions. As a sign of command the exclamation mark
expresses a logically important feature: it singles out a certain type of
sentence, in which there is no question of truth and falsehood, but of
obeying and disobeying. Moreover, the exclamation mark can here
instruct us to complete a fragmentary sentence of command. For example
'John!' = 'John, come here!' Sometimes this mark stands at the end of
sentences that express a state of mind, for example 'alas!' sometimes the
mark in writing (or stress in speech) indicates the fact that we have to do

with a sentence and not a concept; as when someone calls out 'Fire!',
thereby showing that what is meant is not the concept, but the sentence
'fire has broken out'.

(9) From these examples we see that punctuation can have various
meanings and thus must be regarded as ambiguous.

17. TITLES

(1) A title is a fragmentary sentence to be completed according to its
position insofar as the language contains a corresponding sentence
meaning the same but involving more concepts in general use. (See 11).

(2) From the author's point of view, it depends whether the writer
has fixed the title *before* writing the book, so that it amounts to the
sentence 'I will write about...'; or *after* partly or wholly writing it,
which would translate into 'Herein I have written about...'. But since
titles are aimed at the reader and the author later turns into a reader,
the sentence (title) means 'This book is about...' where the 'is' denotes
the time from the writing until all exemplars have perished; that is,
'whoever reads this book while it is a book will find that it is about...'
The title expresses this fact.

(3) For titles that characterize whole sets of sentences, see Part Two,
IV, 7.

18. NOTES ON THE RULES OF RHETORIC AND POETRY

(1) The rules of rhetoric, as current even in antiquity, are advice on how
to influence or persuade the public. But they may be taken also as
psychological observations stating that if someone speaks in certain
ways in certain situations he will influence his audience. Similar 'rules'
exist in chess too, for irritating or otherwise influencing one's opponent:
not to be confused with the proper rules of chess, which are rules of the
game.

(2) The rules of poetry and metre may likewise be discribed as psychological observations, if they are translated somewhat as follows: if the
poem is written in such and such ways, it will be effective and please.
But they must generally be construed as commands, because they request
poets to obey them. However, those sentences concerning metre that
describe the various types of rhyme or sequences of rise and fall and so on,

are sentences just as in zoology or botany; except that here the topic is the spoken word. They have nothing to do with *logical* rules.

(3) Likewise for the rules governing conventions of politeness (the tone of good breeding): either they are descriptions or commands, with a certain section of society acting as the source of command. The sentences contained in a polite formula must be regarded as being *in brackets*. If someone says 'I am sorry' this would mostly turn out to be false if tested as it stands. But if somewhere the expression 'I am sorry' has not taken root and someone uses it even when he feels no sorrow, then he would be lying, since now we should admit immediate testing.

(4) As to rhetorical turns of phrase, the sentences used by the orator may be assertions, commands, wishes, requests, proofs and so on. Being uttered in such a connection, they receive a special index, namely that they must not be taken seriously. What matters is their triggering function. Therefore all these sentences appear as expressions 'in brackets', the word 'rhetoric' is their characteristic and key. Likewise with appeals, publicity, advertising and so on. All these sentences have such indices because the special convention holds both for the writer and the reader.

(5) It is as though the sentence was prefaced by 'I surmise' and the hearer no longer counts on it with certainty, or a sentence begins with 'I hope' and the like. Such sentences will be denoted as being in brackets, these latter differing in nature from case to case.

CHAPTER II

KINDS OF WORDS

1. PROPER NAMES AND GENERAL NAMES

(1) In our language, forming proper names involves using psychological facts such as the experience of similarities, memories and so on. The convention is that the use of the sign is independent of the person's position in space and time. If yesterday's John no longer were today's, nor John in the next room John in this, or John in one suit John in another and so on, I could not call out: 'John, bring me a glass of water!' For at each point I should have to lay down a new convention and tell him of it.

(2) To start, we distinguish two kinds of proper names: (i) where a person simply is given a name; (ii) where the name is determined by one or more systems. Fingerprints are an example of a single system leading to unambiguous identity: 'the man with such and such lines' is a proper name. If everybody carried a unique and unremovable such sign on his face, this alone would suffice for giving this second kind of proper name. But as this is not so, one uses many systems until the proper name is fixed fairly precisely. The expression: 'the man who was standing at the corner on Sunday morning, tall and wearing yellow gloves, and so on' consists of such systems and results in fixing the name.

(3) In a passport several systems are combined (i) the assigned given and family names (one seeks to meet the inconvenience that many people are called John by indicating the family names or the names of father, son and so on since men die and new ones are born, the danger is in any case smaller, so that one need not go on inventing new names). (ii) Place and time of birth, (iii) Description, according to many systems: colour of eyes, height, special marks and so on (these data correct each other and thus tend in the direction of the ideal case).

(4) The difference between assigned names and those fixed by systems lies in the former being in a certain sense simple and the latter composite, and in another sense the reverse. The assigned name is simple in that

its parts are not concepts, but merely letters; whereas the system based name consists of parts that are themselves concepts. Conversely 'John' is composite insofar as it combines many systems (for instance as father of Jack, fairhaired and so on).

(5) A proper name can be represented as a *selection* of points in systems and, if of the first kind, an *abbreviation* for the selected points as well. The usual systems are place, time, height, shape of skull, dress, language and so on. (A radio message describing a missing person to listeners ignorant of the correlation of name and person is by *selection* only. Abbreviation is here at first inapplicable.)

(6) One might ask whether there are proper names of things that do not exist. Since the name was represented as a selection of points each of which belongs to a system, amongst them spatio-temporal ones, the very formation seems to include existence. However, this spatio-temporal system may have another significance, for instance fabulous creatures. 'The virtuous act of Mr. X on such and such a date' is a proper name, even though X may be imaginary. In the question whether Homer existed, 'Homer' is a proper name, although precisely this sentence casts doubt on his existence.

(7) Many sentences consist in correlating the two kinds of proper names: Shakespeare is the author of 'Hamlet'. Here a point of a system is correlated to the name (abbreviation). Someone might ask: since the author of Hamlet is Shakespeare, how can the combination of words just mentioned represent a sentence (in the history of literature), whereas the sentence 'Shakespeare = Shakespeare' is trivial. The answer is that the former conveys a correlation of corresponding points in the system of personal names and the system of authors of plays (it may be analyzed into simpler sentences: Shakespeare wrote the play exemplars of which are spread far and wide, and...); but 'Shakespeare = Shakespeare' conveys nothing. At best it may serve as an example of the law of identity (see Part Two, I, 6).

(8) One might ask: what about a dead person who retains the name John? As abbreviation for his corpse one can use the sign 'John'. But in this new use it belongs to a new part of speech, as is shown by the fact that sentences like 'John is walking' or 'John is thinking' are now inadmissible; such formations are here grammatically barred, just as is the expression 'living corpse' unless used in a metaphorical sense.

The sign 'dead' excludes life and allows only sentences asserted about an inanimate object. The barred sentences amount to 'the non-walking is walking' or 'the non-thinking is thinking'.

(9) Often all we know about a name is some points of the system, many others remaining unknown to us. Not even about ourselves do we know all the important systems. One might take as the decisive elements in forming our proper name items like graphs of weight, growth, temperature. We could hardly give our own name in this fashion, nor, fortunately, do we need to. With historical figures we often know very few of the systems. Sometimes we know a few points of a system but not the 'name'. This happens in cases like Deutero-Isaiah, Pseudo-Plutarch, whose style, mentality and approximate country and epoch we do know, but not the name, that is the abbreviation used at the time. Thus, proper names are and can be very fragmentary.

(10) With general names, the selection of points in systems is different: here one takes a few systems and treats the selection as an instance or type. Here, objects are not examined as to identity but as to sufficiently close similarity to the prototype: if an object satisfies this demand then it belongs to that general name. We are concerned with types formed from systems of selection for the purpose of comparison. We disregard not only John-today, John-tomorrow and so on, but also place and time of birth, racial characteristics and so on, and thus we obtain the concept 'man'. The psychological facts of memory, experience of similarity and the like are here used just as with proper names.

(11) What we call a general name is a cross-section of *many* properties. Take for example 'man': x's hands differ from his feet (which cannot grip), he can speak, write, read and so on (each property being given provisionally and subject to mutual correction). Mutual correction and collaboration of many characteristics creates the required practical clarity. 'Speak', 'write' and so on are in turn general names of activities.

(12) General names apply not only to things but also to activities. The word 'walk' is a general name, denoting a kind of activity, disregarding place, time and manner. But it can serve as a proper name, as in 'Mr. X's walking in a certain street in a certain period.' 'The man now standing in front of me and talking' is a proper name, as is his speaking; but speaking as such is a general name.

(13) There seem to be transitions between proper and general names.

Logically speaking, however, a sharp line must be drawn here: nothing can be both at once, for as soon as the difference is grasped they exclude each other logically. The apparent transition hinges on differences in point of view and ambiguities of one and the same sign. 'The policeman at Charing Cross' is a proper name for traffic but a general name for the authorities (it must be further specified to become a proper name).

(14) 'The uniform of British Rail' is a general name, although one that is more narrowed down and hedged with restrictions. But 'the people now in this room' is a proper name. Using genus and difference one remains in the field of general names, without ever reaching proper names. Between the two there is an unbridgeable gap.

(15) But suppose there were some animal represented by one *single* exemplar, and someone called it 'snark,', would this be a proper name or a general name? It depends on the definition: the former, if the name is to apply only to this one creature even if a second one of the same species turned up; the latter, if the name is to apply to any additional exemplars. One might even stipulate that the name should be proper now and general later. If, however, I asserted that the name was general, even though it is to denote only *this* exemplar, then my language is confused.

(16) A borderline case of a proper name is the 'snapshot'; that is, a sign for a thing, activity or situation for a moment. (Language has no such signs; for its signs are coins; and coins that can be used for only a moment cannot be used as coins.) Usual proper names may be taken as 'chains' of snapshots. The gaps in the chains are hypothetically filled. Such a chain is called the 'history' of the object. The proper name can be used only so long as this chain succeeds in hanging together (so long as we recognize the bearer). For the grammar of general names the opposite holds: a snapshot is grammatically barred. General names have no 'history'; to fill in the gaps by hypotheses would be senseless.

(17) My uncle John; the oldest man in London; the largest city in the world, and the like are proper names. The last two are examples of a method of fixing that transforms general into proper names, which involves a change in grammatical field. In the first example, one must avoid turning the proper name into a general one. Proper names of this kind too can be precise or inadequate according to context: I might have two uncles called John; there might be two coeval Londoners older

than any others or two equally large cities larger than any others.

(18) General names do not apply to themselves: the general name man is not a man. This is so obvious that a sentence like 'man is man' in the sense of 'the concept man is itself a man' cannot occur in ordinary language. However for some words this rule does *not* hold: the word 'word' is itself a word, and likewise the concept 'concept'.

(19) Part of the rules of general names is that one of higher order (a general name of general names) cannot be an element of one of lower order. But only some general names have a steplike structure (for them the vetoes of Russell's theory of types apply). Most general names are not steplike, and even with those where one distinguishes higher and lower steps, three steps at most are formed (beware of generalisations!). There could of course be motives leading to steplike structures for all general names, so that these rules would apply everywhere. For steplike general names the rule of genus and difference applies, but only for them and not, as used to be held, for every kind of word.

One must indeed guard against generalizing the grammar of any *one* kind of word or sentence. The ancients, by wrongly thinking everywhere of general names of different degrees, were led to their well-known explanation of definition by genus and difference. The same holds of the syntactic error of many exponents of mathematical logic who treat all sentences as assertions. There are many words and sentences that have an aura of universality, but remember the *other* kinds of words and sentences.

(20) Man and milk are general names insofar as they satisfy those conditions that have been mentioned in contrast with proper names. But they differ as to grammar. The parts of so-called mass nouns (milk, silver and so on), being homogeneous, can be distinguished only as to weight, location and so on. (Chemical structure does not belong here.) The name 'lion' applies to the whole kind as well as to each member, but each individual can easily be marked by a proper name, for they usually differ in colour, build, and so on. In a circus, for example, each lion receives a name of his own. That this is not *always* so hinges on the fact that we are usually no interested in the individual life history of each lion. If one tries to do the same with silver, it turns out to be rather clumsy. But since proper names would there be out of place, one simply forgoes them and so reaches mass nouns: these are general names with

formation of proper names ruled out. If one numbers pieces of silver so that they can be distinguished, then the name silver is a general name like lion, which comprises individuals.

(21) In a certain sense, general names have no plural: men is a plural not of the general name man, but of the several proper names. 'Men' has the same extension as 'man', and similarly for all general names. Thus the plural of general names relates to the elements that belong to them; in contrast with mass nouns, which lack such elements.

2. EXAMPLES OF NAMES MADE MORE SPECIFIC AND PRECISE

(1) *Apposition* makes more precise in order to eliminate mistakes: it completes names. Proper names that do not consist of signs that have other uses as well, often require explanation and the relevant convention specifically spelled out. For it is characteristic of linguistic economy that many people are called John, so that proper names have to be amplified by other data. Sometimes, however, apposition signifies specification of the general name, or its transformation into a proper name.

(2) Language has several methods of specifying general names. For example, diminutives: booklet, piglet and the like. Likewise compound names such as apple tree, winter coat and so on. (Attributive combinations such as the possessive case belong here also, see 4.) A language with diminutive forms is richer in expressions than one without, even though 'booklet' may be rendered by 'small book'.

(3) The gender ending *ess* is not a specification of general names. Since 'count' denotes a man, 'countess' is not a subclass (or part of the general name) of 'count', and therefore no specification. If 'book' meant 'big book', then 'booklet' would be no specification, since the two general names would be different.

3. DEFINITE AND INDEFINITE ARTICLE

(1) 'A man is coming from afar; the coat the man wears is dark'. This 'the', in contrast with 'a', relates to the man whom we do not know. Since he has not yet been further described to us in any ordinary sense, why *the*? 'A man' is a general name insofar as one can substitute anybody.

But as soon as the report specifies him and so turns him into a proper name, one rightly uses the definite article, for proper names are given by sets of data and can be more or less definite. Within this tale, if no greater precision is demanded, 'the man who is coming from afar' is already a proper name. So is 'the coat', for the data (wearer, time) turn it from general into proper name.

(2) The difference between definite and indefinite article may be formulated thus: the former mostly marks transformation of general into proper names; the latter, membership of a general name (but not the general name itself). Both, however, have other meanings, some of which will be mentioned later.

(3) One can imagine a language that lacks this distinction, so that no difference is made between a definite stone and just any stone. We do not wish to object that the difference cannot be absent from a language, for it could easily be that the language will yet acquire many systems, so that later generations will be amazed that their forebears could not take into account such obvious differences and will try to interpret them into the language. Likewise it would be wrong to ascribe a difference obvious to us to *every* language.

(4) In conventional grammar it is sometimes stated that in certain cases the definite article may occur before a proper name if separated by an attributive adjective: 'the victorious Wellington', 'the great Newton'. These two differ in logical grammar. In the former case, we pick out a phase in Wellington's history, so that his name really functions as a general name and the whole expression is a proper name; while in the latter case we described the whole scientific career of Newton, so that his name already functions as a proper name and the adjective is really a predicate. The former expression translates into 'Wellington, when victorious', the latter into 'Newton is great'.

(5) The definite article often has no definite meaning so that it is really an *indefinite* article. For example 'he took the knife'. In subsuming sentences (which express that a concept belongs to a group of mutually replaceable concepts) such as 'the horse is an animal', 'the' is the article for the genus 'horse'. Similarly for other kinds of sentences where the definite article relates to a genus; but it never relates to *membership* of the genus.

(6) The indefinite article 'a' contains two things (i) the notion of 'any',

in contrast with proper names (ii) the number 1 in contrast to 'many'. Since mass nouns are not liable to being counted, unless shape enters (see 1), there is no motive for applying numbers. One cannot say '2 waters', '2 meats' unless one means for example two stretches of water or two kinds of meat. Hence the indefinite article, connected with the numerical system 'one–many', cannot be applied to them. There is no call for applying numbers to things where one does not know where the first ends and the second begins.

4. THE GENITIVE CASE (DECLENSION)

(1) The needs of practical life are not such that we might do with only proper or only general names. It would be clumsy to give each man's fingers proper names, since in practice it is of no importance to mark each of them. Insofar as it is important, general names have been formed, for example thumb, index, ring-finger and so on.

(2) A special name for Mr. X's thumb is superfluous. Since the person already has a name and thumbs their general name, one has refrained from giving his thumb a special name. If our hands were not privileged over our feet, many fingers would lack names, just like the toes. That certain parts of the body have special anatomical names does not contradict our view, but confirms it, for in anatomy it happens to matter; besides, they are all general names, since proper ones do not matter there either. No one will think of marking each individual hair in the manner of fingers. But if some science were to concern itself with the minutest detail of hair, it would introduce many new names, as anatomy does for individual nerves. Everday language has its adequate names. The sign 'thumb' is enough for all thumbs, but not the sign 'man' for Tom, Dick and Harry. If it were, Tom would have no name. If we are concerned with a thumb, we are usually not greatly interested (except in fingerprinting and the like, but even there it is the owner and not the peculiarity of the thumb that interests us); but if someone says 'a person has come', we would like to learn something about him. That is why people have their proper names, and thumbs and hair not.

(3) To distinguish Mr. X's thumb from others, if necessary, one proceeds by means of another system of reference. For example, Mr. X's thumb. This could be a system of kinship, property, descent and so on,

and that is the function of the genitive which specifies general names turning them into proper names.

(4) The material of the genitive is often used outside genitive situations. For example, in German, the preposition 'wegen' (=because of) *governs* the genitive, although the genitive function is not involved. In a critical grammar we should not find the statement about governing, but rather this: the preposition 'wegen' is followed by material that is normally used for the genitive.

(5) If the property relation is used to specify a general name, we have a possessive genitive, which serves to make both general and proper names more precise. If translated (analyzed), a complex sentence is replaced by a sentence indicating ownership. For example 'X's garden is next to Y's' translates into 'X has a garden and Y has a garden and...' Similarly for the other kinds of genitive using other systems.

(6) As to the other cases (of declension), the nominative (like the infinitive of the verb) is the proper form of the concept; that is, as listed in the dictionary, disregarding functions within a sentence. On the accusative case, see Part One, III, 2. About declension as such we here note merely that the word 'declension' is a misleading description. If we compare the above account of genitive function with the earlier one of accusative function, we see that declension comprises quite disparate matter.

(7) Every case is marked by some small change of the material: mensa, mensam, and so on. The fact that the form mensae stands for both genitive and dative seems an inappropriate economy. There are many such examples. Just as it is clumsy to use the same material to denote different objects and activities, so it seems inappropriate to use the same materials to denote different grammatical functions.

5. FABULOUS CREATURES AND IMAGINARY CONCEPTS

(1) A series of general names like 'unicorn', 'griffin', 'dragon' and the like have changed their linguistic location in the course of time. When men believed reports on such creatures, the names were general, like 'lion', 'elephant' and so on. If the story was about a dragon, one meant an individual belonging to a kind about which various things were known. The statements might be verified, for everyone could become

acquainted with one of these beasts. But once one had gone over to explaining such statements differently than on the basis of direct perceptions, the concepts were transferred from the domain of other general names of animals to the domain of fable and imaginary general names: a new convention was laid down for them. If St. George came home and said 'I met a dragon' this was logically just as sound as saying 'I met a Syrian'. If today someone comes home and says 'I met a dragon', using present day language, he has offended against grammar, unless he meant it metaphorically. But if he meant a creature that answers to the ancient reports, he would have to analyse thus: 'I wish to use the concept of 'dragon' the way the ancients did and I met a dragon'. The sentence contains a report and a linguistic reform. (That this change was occasioned by a certain experience is self-evident; for that is the way of all concept formation.)

(2) If historians were to explain stories about Napoleon as the product of a lively imagination and their view became accepted (so that language forced them to lay down a new convention about this concept, which in this case seems unlikely for the time being), the fate of this proper name would resemble that of the general names just mentioned: it would undergo a change of location.

(3) But wherein consists this change? Put differently: what is the difference between Napoleon and Hamlet in present day language? The answer is: the method of verification of sentences containing these concepts. For example, in 1809 Napoleon was in Aspern near Vienna. Given the current meaning of the proper name, this sentence should turn out true or false on the basis of documents and their comparison, it being irrelevant whether anyone hitherto knew the fact or not: Napoleon might have been there unnoticed. But if we adopted the above historical phantasy, or if we examine the sentence 'Hamlet was in Aspern in 1809' we must examine whether at some time this was believed, whether people were of the opinion that it was such and such. (In the case of Hamlet, for example, whether the author had asserted this of him.) If someone asserted that Napoleon (in his usual meaning) had been somewhere, though unnoticed both then and later, the assertion remains true. For the fictitious Napoleon such an assertion is senseless: for only if people at some time believed it of him can the assertion be true. The sense of the sentence would be: people believed that 'Napoleon' was at such and such a place in the year x.

(4) When the historian in quest for such a person tries to solve the question 'did x exist?', x so far lacks a definite linguistic location. Therefore he tries to use *both* methods of verification, and in this case takes on the linguistic task at the same time; he tries to range the concept, in order to give the sentences containing it precise sense and so subject them to the appropriate method of verification.

(5) Human vocabulary is not fixed. Words change their location according to the sentences formed and their sense. The view that the meanings of words are fixed once and for all often leads to confusion. The observation of changes in logical location is particularly important for the understanding of language.

6. SUBJECT AND SUBSTANTIVE

(1) Within the field of asserting sentences there is a group that have attained a dominating role, namely subject-predicate sentences.

(2) These are formed when the connections to be conveyed are represented by choosing one part as bearer and attaching all the rest to it. Grammar calls this bearer subject.

(3) If someone wants to report 'over there lies a green leaf', this can be done in various ways. For example: 'green, there, leaf, lying'; or 'leaf, green, lie, there', 'green leaf lies there' and all the other variations (compare the most varied sequences in the various types of language).

(4) The difference between 'over there lies a green leaf' and 'a green leaf lies over there', and so on, in our language is that the first is stressed on 'there', the second on 'green', according to what the assertion mainly refers to (place or colour), that is, which system is emphasized. (The sequence here often has the function of stress.) But if this was the criterion in ascertaining subject and predicate, then the accent on 'green' to exclude other colours would make *that* word the subject (which would thus migrate with stress). However, the bearer should be constant.

(5) From all these equally admissible ways of grouping the concepts we therefore choose the one that in its elementary form gives to one sign the privileged position of basic sign. (The elementary form of the sentence is one in which it cannot be dismantled into two or more sentences. In the present example, we would have 'a leaf is over there and that leaf is green'.) To begin with it is the object that is more perma-

nent, that is a cross-section that is invariant as to colour, position and the like, and not susceptible to degree. This simply lies in our convention that the green object on this or that tree, so long as it has a certain likeness in form or touch (also if it is yellow and half withered, lying away from the tree), is still to be called 'leaf'. That is why we have nominated it as subject.

(6) We might also have chosen the other way: the green is leaf. We could thus have chosen a member of a simple system (see Part Two, I, 3) as bearer of the sentence. For nominating a certain kind of sign as bearer makes no difference to the sentence.

(7) Putting *one* object into the centre somehow answers a human need: a house is more permanent, while the furniture varies; some parts of the body are more protected than others. The vessel in which water is kept; the stove in which fire is kept and the like are specially distinguished.

(8) Usually it is a cross-section that becomes the subject of a sentence. What in syntax is called subject is called substantive in accidence. This applies only to certain kinds of sentence, for instance of the type thing-activity, thing-feeling and the like. This 'prerogative' is extended to activities, as in 'walking is healthy', the activity becoming a substantive and so able to function as subject. There are other groups of sentences in which substantive and subject do not coincide. For examples sentences in the first person and relational sentences: (i) I am walking, (ii) *a* loves *b*. In (i) the subject is not a substantive, in (ii) *b* is substantive but not subject.

(9) A certain misuse of the subject which is grammatically irrelevant anyway consists in *the search for the subject*, which claims many grammarians as victims. Blinded by the prejudice that every sentence must always have a subject, they analyse sentences like 'it is raining', '*a* loves *b*', as follows: 'it' ('*a*') is the subject, 'is raining' ('loves *b*') the predicate. Grammarians here need to ponder their actions.

(10) Signs liable to degree, such as 'slowness', have also been made into substantives. The ending in English, however explained etymologically, is a sign of adjective turned substantive. In this way such a word may even become subject, that is be made the pivot of a sentence. Abbreviations for modes of behaviour, like 'virtue', or abbreviations for differences in such modes, like 'death', are also such transformations.

(11) If many parts of speech can be made substantive, what is a substantive? One might say: whatever can become a subject. But this

role of subject is a fortuitous feature of certain languages. One could turn space time coordinates into subjects, so that the spatial or temporal word becomes subject and all else is attached to it. Turning words into substantives is grammatically important, whereas the role of subject is merely a requirement of style. One wants to know *about what* one is speaking, just as one wants a container into which one can put everything.

(12) In the earlier sentence 'over there lies a green leaf' anything may become subject, according to the convention adopted as to what should receive the privileged position of bearer. But turning a word into a substantive is grammatically significant: 'lying' differs from 'lie' in that the former is not answerable to changes of time; likewise 'green' is not capable of degrees of comparison. Turning a word into a substantive is a grammatical change of location; for although 'green' remains a colour name, and 'lying' a mode of behaviour, they have become general names that possess totality. Now they can be turned into *proper names* as well: 'leaf x's lying at a given place at a given time', 'the green here or there', and so on.

(13) What, then, is a substantive? Does it perhaps comprise kinds of words as different as tree, life, walking, green and so on? What justifies their common name? The answer lies in the grammar of proper and general names. To turn into a substantive means to use in the sense of the definitions valid for proper and general names (amongst them the vetoes on comparing, conjugating in time, and so on).

(14) The ending 'ness' in 'slowness' marks the veto on comparison and the possibility of forming a proper name. Similarly for strong and strength: the former can be compared, the latter not. Turned substantive, this word becomes the sign of the system strong–weak. One can speak of the strength of a weak object, because 'strength' means 'strong or weak'. If the attributive expression 'the strength of this object' is used in a sentence, it is not to be translated into an independent sentence 'this object is strong', for the object might be weak.

(15) If one speaks of a stone's hardness, one disregards all degrees. Hardness is the word for the system hard–soft.

(16) We can justify the term 'substantive' by saying that it denotes proper and general names, systems and collections; indeed all signs whose scope can be restricted or widened but which cannot be compared or conjugated. The term does not denote a uniform system of substitu-

tions, but comprises quite different parts of speech: people, other animals, inanimate objects, activities (with or without indication of purpose or value), places (with or without regard to population and so on), periods (with or without regard to what happens in them), arrangements, processes, states, modes of behaviour, differences in these modes, grammatical signs, and so on. To denote this only sketchy list by the uniform term 'substantive' is unjustified insofar as it tends to make one ignore the many bars to substitution that are involved and so to overlook the differences between the signs.

7. THE ADJECTIVE

(1) The common feature that leads to the name adjective rests on the fact that all the attendant systems of signs consist of a few elements each of which has three degrees (of comparison). But this holds also of other signs that are not usually counted as adjectives. Thus the system much-little, each element unfolds into a system of three members: much, more, most; little, less, least.

(2) The systems we call adjectives, and those related to them arise from *the need to compare*: one *opposes* the beautiful to the ugly, the good to the bad, the light to the dark and so on. If one further observes differences in shade within the elements being compared, one obtains a three step system (which could equally have two or many steps, see Part One, III, 5); combining opposition and scale of degree, we obtain an adjective (that some adjectives are not complete is obvious).

(3) The domain in which the system of comparison is used must have upper and lower bounds; it must be fixed, even if vague. A says: 'the smallest object in this room lies on the right'. Suppose B can show that there is a still smaller microscopically discernible speck on the left. Who is right? Both, for they have applied this moveable system to different domains.

(4) That activities, feelings, states and so on are not compared as to shade (for example with 'see': 'see better', 'see worse' and so on) is not given in itself but due to special conventions of language; for verbs, this differentiations is produced in another way, namely by using adjectives which in this special case are called adverbs. But one might well have 'inflected' verbs not only as to time but also as to these degrees.

(5) Comparison within the domain bounded by positive and superlative is called comparative. Comparison thus combines the system in question with the system more–less. One could set up a system in which one operates with 'less' instead of 'more'. We have a special form for *A* higher than *B* in the domain, but not for *A* lower than *B*. For the latter one substitutes the corresponding element of the opposite domain. The systems complement each other.

(6) That the grammatical distinction between indicative and subjunctive is not applied to the system of colour or size (big, bigger, biggest) and so on is a peculiarity of the way our language is formed. One could easily introduce forms for 'certainly blue' (or big) and 'not quite certainly blue'. If language made this distinction, one could form the subjunctive of predicate sentences (that is ones that have no finite verb other than the copula, such as 'this is blue') without using auxiliary expressions like 'it seems' and the like. In such sentences the difference moreover shows in the auxiliary verb 'to be'. This *is* so; whether this *be* so or not ... The 'is' here signifies the correspondence between definite points (see Part Two, III, 13) and indicates the certainty or otherwise of the correlation. The systems themselves, however, are to stand outside this difference.

(7) The words that belong to this part of speech can take on a metric. But there must be a prior point of purchase. Saying 'the tree is tall' presupposes that one knows already when one would say small. Otherwise it would be senseless to speak of a tall tree. Likewise with fast–slow. The first indication, however, is not supplied by a metric, rather it supplies the standard of comparison.

(8) The word 'tall' in '30 ft tall' is not the first degree of comparison, but an indication of dimension: not long, not wide, but tall. Without measure, 'tall' denotes both dimension and approximate height; with measure, it denotes only dimension. Used without measure, 'tall' is moreover a concept that belongs to the system tall–small, so that it makes sense to substitute 'small'; but in '30 ft tall' we cannot substitute 'small', because this 'tall' no longer belongs to tall–small.

(9) 'This table is 30 ft longer than that one'. The 'long' in 'longer' here signifies both dimension and comparison. But in 'this table is long' one intends comparison; one can contradict it by 'the table is short'. One must distinguish between 'long' from long–short (or 'wide' from wide–narrow) and 'long' from the triple system long–wide–high.

(10) If dimension had been fixed once and for all, so that one would have to use a compass to discover what is length or width, it would be clear that 'long' in the sense of dimension is different from 'long' in the sense of comparison. But such a convention would be impractical, since it would all hinge on an object that is not always present. Not so with height, because our own posture always helps to determine it: because we walk erect, this direction is so familiar to us that determination of the heights of all objects in our surroundings suits us best. (One might of course regard outstretched arms as length and the direction front to back as width and so determine dimensions. But this would be clumsy since our body constantly changes its direction. Therefore the convention has been laid down that both directions are first compared without dimension and then the longer is called length.) Long, wide and high in the sense of dimension have no degrees of comparison; in the sense of comparison they have.

(11) As to comparison of colour names, if they already include all shades, they cannot be compared; as for instance when one speaks generally of the colours blue, black and so on. Here black is intended as against green, blue and so on, and not a particular shade of black. For all shades of black have been given this name as against green. But if within the domain of black one compares two different shades, one is using a new system, and in certain circumstances it is the system of degrees of comparison. Black as against green, good as against bad, mean something different from black as against blacker, good as against better. Within the system of degrees they mean not so black (or good).

(12) The expression 'adjective' (thrown alongside) is justified insofar as the relevant systems are set alongside the most varied signs in various areas. For example 'big' can be applied to tables, achievements, people; 'good' to shoes, character and so on. As a result they are highly ambiguous. For while with a word like 'box' there are areas of vagueness in which 'forces' such as purpose and shape are in mutual conflict, with many an adjective one cannot even speak of vagueness until it has been set alongside a word.

(13) Comparing of distances, bodies and the like, often takes place in memory or imagination. It is therefore wrong to think that introducing a metric would make the triple system big–bigger–biggest redundant. If in my imagination I want to compare my walks of yesterday and

today, I need such a system. If one abandoned it, the language would be the poorer to that extent. Likewise in many similar cases.

(14) If two people argue, A saying 'this picture is beautiful' and B 'this picture is not beautiful' (or A 'this man is good' and B 'this man is bad' and the like), the disputants ought to agree what (approximately at least) is to be denoted as beautiful (in pictures) or good (in people), so that they can ascertain whether they are arguing about grammar or about facts. If the former, they would do well to introduce $good_1$ and $good_2$, which removes terminological troubles and often reveals that they are not really contradicting each other. If the latter, each had best indicate as precisely as possible what method of verification he has used. Much dispute could be got out of the way in this manner. It is as though two people were arguing about whether a table in the house next door is big or small. If they agree to introduce a metric, say up to 30 ft = small, anything beyond = big, that finishes the grammatical side. If the will is there, one can always agree on grammatical questions. If *after* fixing the terminology one cannot agree whether X is good or bad, the table big or small, one can adjourn until further evidence turns up.

8. PREDICATIVE AND ATTRIBUTIVE FORM OF THE ADJECTIVE

(1) Considering the difference between predicatively and attributively connecting adjective with substantive one is at first inclined to take it in the same way as the difference between a sentence of grammar and one of applied language: attributive adjectives restrict names and thus remain within the domain of concepts, whereas predicative adjectives mark a certain type of sentence in applied language.

(2) However, closer examination shows that the sentences 'the green leaf is lying on the right' and 'this leaf is green' differ in that the former is complex and contains the latter: that alone is the difference between attribute and predicate.

(3) In Latin, all adjectives agree with their substantives in gender, number and case: this is a superfluous carefulness of language! In German, only attributive adjectives agree, in English, adjectives are invariable. Does a Latin sentence translated into English suffer any change by this difference? By no means, some languages simply discard such agreement. It is not as if one translates from a language that has a perfect

tense into one that has not, so that special words (circumlocutions) must be enlisted to achieve the same result.

9. VAGUE AND METRIC SYSTEMS

(1) There are words that presuppose a numerical system of measurement such as: threefold, four-fold, 1 ft, 1 m and the like; others presuppose a vague system of measurement, such as: fast, slow, high, deep, wide, long, where numerical scales are yet to be introduced. These latter systems will be called vague, the former metric.

(2) An example of a vague system is the two term system often–seldom; it relates to the distribution of events or activities within a temporal area, but can apply also to distribution in space and to other situations (within the system often–seldom one uses moreover degrees of comparison: often, oftener, oftenest; seldom, more seldom, most seldom. *A* occurs oftener than *B*' can be expressed the other way round: '*B* occurs more seldom than *A*'.) For things one uses 'many' and 'few', a vague system, too.

(3) But even where numbers are used (in metric systems) one can proceed in different ways: if some one has a pile of fruit, of which he wants to give one third to his friend, he can count the pieces and divide the number by three; or he can put them into three equal containers, or weigh out three equal portions. In all three cases he has used the number series, combining it with the systems many–few and heavy–light in cases one and three respectively, obtaining three results each of which is to be denoted independently of the others as one third.

10. EXAMPLES OF DISPLACEABLE SYSTEMS

(1) With pronouns we shall meet some systems that have the property of being attachable to various areas. At present let us examine displaceable systems through some other examples. (The systems in question consist of few elements, like the above vague systems, whereas metric systems using basic number words have a beginning but no end.) Here–there: here by the table, there by the door; here at home, there abroad. Likewise above–below, before–after–at the same time, and so on.

(2) In many specializations of language where it matters to make

systems like above–below, forwards–backwards, undisplaceable, less ambiguous expressions have been introduced; such as 'cranial', 'dorsal', 'ventral' instead of above, at the back, in front, and the like in anatomy.

(3) Any such indication must have a point of departure (or purchase): if I say 'next week', then *this* week must have been fixed. If I say 'left', then the place concerned must be given and so on. The reference points may be fixed vaguely or more precisely (metrically). They are displaceable insofar as they can be applied anywhere.

(4) 'Simultaneously–before–after' is a displaceable system with the point of reference 'simultaneously': this fixed, the others can be found. The system presupposes at least two events which can be related provided the point of reference is fixed. For example: people in a pub are playing snooker at two tables. If simultaneity has not been fixed, one cannot denote the balls on one table as moving earlier or later than those on the other; this requires prior definition of simultaneous motion on the two tables.

(5) Outside–inside. This system is used also metaphorically, in which case it loses its spatial meaning, as in combinations like 'inner life', 'inner sense' and the like.

(6) To walk *towards–away from*. This system concerns direction of motion once a point has been fixed.

(7) On the near side–far side: the place concerned is devided into two parts by a borderline or strip, which is the point of reference. A certain local area is intended: the country beyond the Channel does not mean places on other planets. (Metaphors like 'life beyond' must be translated.)

(8) Above–below: prepositionally, this does not assume the speaker as point of reference; adverbially it does (like outside–inside).

(9) This, too, is the place of the system near–far, and the signs 'between', 'next to', 'opposite to', 'alongside', and so on.

(10) We must distinguish systems that contain the reference point as one member, such as here–there, from others that do not, such as above–below prepositionally.

11. EXAMPLES OF INDEFINITE SIGNS

(1) There are situations in which one cannot say precisely who has done

something, although one suspects that somebody did. Language has evolved special forms for this: '*They* have done it', '*somebody* has done it' and the like. The scope of such concepts is wide, for the sentence remains true whoever did it; but not *always*, so that the sentence conveys something. Such signs do have their function, amongst other things they convey ignorance as to more precise data. (Our language has been designed for the human condition, so that we should lose a lot if just these indefinite words were lacking.)

(2) By 'somebody' we mean membership of the general name 'man'. The opposite is 'nobody'. 'One' often means 'some, or many, people not further specifiable'.

(3) 'Something – nothing' is related to things, activities and so on, not to people. 'Never–ever' is a temporal system that becomes triple with 'sometimes' or 'occasionally'. With 'again', 'once more' one uses the numerical system n and $n+1$ (a two term numerical system applied to events) 'Everybody' can be linked with 'somebody' and 'nobody'.

(4) Where the agent is unknown, one often uses the passive: 'this person has been shot'. Such sentences resemble problems (equations) with unknowns. (We are not going to forego expressing what we do know because we lack other data.)

(5) 'Somebody has injured the animal' implies that some other living thing has done the injuring; 'the animal has been injured' implies that we do not know this, and thus that we know less.

(6) Sentences containing indefinite signs are true or false just as other sentences: 'somehow some such event occurred somewhere near here' is either true or false. That a sentence has greater scope, is very often true and consists of vague signs, does not alter the rule that an assertion is either true or false.

12. PRONOUNS

Personal Pronouns

(1) The system of personal pronouns divides all persons (men) into three groups (as with activities and feelings in respect of time), the point of reference always needing to be fixed: the speaker is 'I', the addressed is 'you', all others are third persons.

(2) It is not as with the system of proper names where each retains his own. 'I', 'you', 'he' are variables for the entire language, like x, y, z.

But if one has fixed the reference point and then wishes to compare the system with that of proper names, 'I', for me, retains the one meaning. But 'you' changes: sometimes it becomes 'he' and conversely.

(3) 'We' is an abbreviation for 'I and others'. Thus 'we are walking' = 'I am walking and the others are (or he is) walking'. 'We' is not the plural of 'I', for part of the grammar of 'I' is a veto on plural formation. Only because all the others that are walking use the same three term system I–you–he and each of them says 'I am walking' in such a situation does 'we are walking' appear to be the *plural* of 'I am walking'. 'We are in pain', 'we rejoice' are logically complex sentences belonging to various types: 'I am in pain' signifies an experience, 'John is in pain' is an abbreviation for modes of behaviour.

(4) 'To remember' is a two term system: someone remembers something (or somebody), the object being an accusative. In German the corresponding verb takes the genitive, which really offends against logical grammar: the sign 'genitive' tacitly assumes another function. It might be called a kind of accusative.

(5) The term *pro nomen* seems to be appropriate in some cases. For insofar as proper or general names have already occurred in a conversation, one simply uses the pronoun in place of the name. But deputizing is not the essential feature of pronouns, being neither their sole nor most important functions. If one imagines a language lacking the system I–you–he, more than abbreviations would be missing. A language could have the system of personal pronouns yet lack proper names. Inessential features of pronouns have been unduly stressed.

(6) If every person called himself John and all others Jack, just as in fact one uses 'I' and 'he', proper names would have been abolished: personal pronouns would be alone in the field.

(7) The fact that 'you' translates both into German 'du' and 'Sie' (polite address) shows that the last two are the same as to logical grammar. On closer acquaintance, the polite form gives way to the familiar, without affecting conversation. However, an observer can infer what is the relation between the speakers. This could be amplified by having different forms according to who is speaking to whom, for example, father to son, son to father, doctor to patient and so on.

(8) 'I' refers to people. If this form is used with other animals ('the fox said: I want to ...'), we may proceed in two ways. (i) We translate

their behaviour into human language; it means: if the animal could speak, it could express the matter thus or thus. In this way one can verify the sentence. If a dog makes a certain gesture indicating the desire to go outside and someone comments that the dog means by this 'I want to go outside', the sentence can be verified if one translates it into 'A person of our linguistic sphere would use the sentence: I want to go outside'. (ii) The key of the combination of sentences is 'fable' or 'fairy tale'; see Part Two, IV, 7.

(9) The 'it' of the third person when relating to inanimate objects does not belong to the system of three persons, but is *merely* an abbreviation or *pronomen*.

(10) 'I' has no neuter, nor 'you' or 'he'; except if language were to ignore the difference between animate and inanimate and therefore alter the system accordingly. Since there is no motive for this, the system of three persons is restricted to living beings (mainly people).

(11) 'X is saying that I could remember'. The subjunctive form which would normally be barred is here permissible because 'I' means 'I' for me but 'he' for X. For doubts about one's own present state of mind are senseless. (If someone is asked whether he is glad or not and his answer is accompanied by a dubious expression on his face, the meaning of this sign must not be misconstrued as his being in doubt about his own state; rather, he is afraid that by using ordinary language he may provoke misunderstandings, because language does not have a definite sign for every state.)

Reflexive Pronouns

(1) These arise from combining personal pronouns with the accusative.

(2) Combining 'I–you–he' with '$x\,R\,y$' gives 'me–you–him'; while with '$x\,R\,x$' the result is 'myself – yourself – himself', the reflexives. In the plural we similarly obtain 'us–you–them' and 'ourselves–yourselves–themselves'.

(3) Without reflexives, one cannot see whether in a given case the relation is $x\,R\,x$ or $x\,R\,y$, unless one observes the context (adducing other systems). Introducing reflexives increases grammatical multiplicity. (For the relation symbol 'R' see Part Two, III, 12.)

(4) 'They know each other'. Here the expression 'each other' is a quasi-reflexive. The meaning is, for example, 'a knows b and b knows a',

an instance of $x \, R \, y$ and $y \, R \, x$. Such pronouns are called reciprocals.

(5) Some systems are fragmentary, exhibiting a certain economy in the language that makes do with existing forms and relying on other systems to lead to clarity where required. This is what is meant by saying 'it follows from the context'.

(6) The word 'oneself' in expressions like 'enjoy oneself' is only an apparent reflexive. (In such cases there is really no relation.)

(7) 'I see myself in the mirror'. This is not, as might at first appear, a simple reflexive relation $x \, R \, x$, for the first 'I' means something other than the second. Indeed, the 'I' in 'myself' is vague; in particular it here means my face, for otherwise one would see oneself quite often even when not in front of a mirror. Let the reader now try to formulate the difference.

Possessive Pronouns

(1) These presuppose the system of personal pronouns. Other systems (kinship, property and so on) are combined with personal pronouns to yield proper names: 'my father', 'your house', 'his hand'. (Often this restricts general names without yielding proper ones: 'your house' can be variable since the owner can have several houses.) Language attains proper names through several reference systems. Possessive pronouns are such a composition of systems, namely pronoun and genitive. In predicative sentences, the forms 'mine – yours – his' are used: 'the house is mine'.

(2) In 'my father' or 'your father', the system is indeed well suited to forming proper names, provided we can keep the situation fixed (that is, we know the reference point of the system). Here we use the systems of kinship and pronouns to turn the general name 'father' into a proper name.

(3) 'Your' stands for several systems. If in 'your father' we think of kinship, the choice occurs because 'your' appears with 'father'.

(4) That 'my' occurs in various senses will be clear from the following three expressions that may appear in sentences: (i) 'my feet' in 'I wash my feet'. (ii) 'My tooth' in 'that is my tooth, on the table there'. (iii) 'My ache' in 'my headache prevents me from thinking about it'. In (i) the general name is turned into a proper name by specifying the part of the body as mine: it hangs together with my body and if it were cut I would normally feel it; without it I would walk with difficulty and its movements depend on my will and so on. All this together signifies 'my foot'. But in (ii) the part, though once fulfilling similar conditions, now no longer

does. As a further example we might consider a foot with anaesthetised nerves. The connection with one's body can still be perceived by touch or sight, but some conditions fulfilled by (i) are now lacking. This is the transition to (ii). But in (iii), the meaning of 'my' is quite different, as can be variously made clear. For example: in (i) and (ii) I may at times doubt *whose* foot or tooth it is, but it is senseless to doubt whether it is *my* pain or somebody else's.

(5) Consider the example 'my book', which has two meanings: (i) the book I wrote (ii) the book I bought. The first concerns authorship, the second ownership. Hence 'book' appears in two senses; in (i) the signs of the book are linguistic, for it remains 'the author's book' whatever sort of paper or ink and so on were used; in (ii) 'the book means the leaves, ink and so on. If I have lent somebody the book in sense (ii), I can ask him to return it, whereas I cannot lend him the book in sense (i).

(6) 'Your picture' can mean three things: (i) the picture you painted, (ii) the picture that represents you, (iii) the picture you own; by mutual interference these can occasion misunderstandings. Possessive pronouns fall into many groups. What they have in common is merely what was said about the grammar of the genitive combined with personal pronouns. These 'possessive' words are called pronouns because their logical translation always involves I, you or he.

(7) If a sentence contains the expression 'my X', this must be analyzed into the predicative sentence 'X is mine'. Hence any complex sentence in which the concept X is attributively linked with 'my' contains amongst other things that predicative sentence.

Demonstrative Pronouns

(1) This system is two term and serves to fix the points in space, time, series and so on. 'This (one)' and 'that (one)' are called pronouns although they have nothing to do with the three term system of personal pronouns. They resemble it in that both sets of signs can replace proper names.

(2) Some systems in language are, as previously mentioned, adequate for primitive conditions where our demands for accuracy remain modest; but where accuracy matters they often appear inadequate. 'This-that', too, is a system that can be most useful in circumscribed situations, though unable to cope with the demands of more developed ones. To describe the trees in the whole wood, it is not enough to say 'this tree'

and 'that tree'; but if only two trees matter, one of them bearing fruit and the other not, one standing near-by and the other further off, then the demonstratives will do.

(3) The point of reference of this system is usually indicated by pointing: This tree... (pointing in a certain direction), that tree (pointing elsewhere, if many other surrounding trees are being considered but excluded by this second reference; without gesture if only two trees can be intended, so that the second reference is superfluous because speaker and hearer use the same two term system). Thus the system has been applied in a special case. It resembles a technical device, a screw or a light globe delivered from the factory to the place where it is wanted: now it can be used. (Note the three stages: making, delivering, using.)

(4) The moment we leave, the whole system vanishes like magic. It is like the system front–back for orientation in space. For the immediate occasion, the system would be quite adequate, but for our requirements and 'permanent language' it cannot be used out of context with other systems. ('Permanent language' is anything not confined to the immediate message; a story, for instance, would qualify.) The signs 'front–back' or 'this–that' can relate to a sentence where a system like 'north–south–east–west', 'at the peak–at the foot of the mountain' and so on have already been applied; in such cases these signs are again used as if someone stood in a certain spot and used 'front–back', or if he said 'this' or' that' while pointing.

(5) It is left to the reader to try to describe the function of the other pronouns (relative, interrogative). Do these function as pronouns in the same sense as personal pronouns?

The ambiguity of the word 'it'. Some of the various senses of this sign (i) 'personal pronoun' for neuters in the third person singular. (ii) Standing for sentences under discussion as in 'I know it'; the 'it' may be explained before or after the event: 'It is well that...', 'I suspect it'. (iii) A variable, as in 'it is my father' $= x$ is a (x variable and a constant). (iv) 'It is raining', 'it is snowing' and the like ('impersonal' pronoun); the 'it' serves to denote pseudo-activities with verbs relating to events.

13. Some remarks on number words

(1) The sign '0' is the 'beginning' of the number series, the point of

reference of the number system. If in some language that system lacks zero, then the point of reference is '1'. For a displaceable and universally applicable system must have a reference point if it is to be used. The number system can have *an end*; as is indeed the case with many primitive tribes: for example, they might not distinguish between 100, 101, 102 and so on. But in our language, too, alongside the number series that can be infinitely extended, there are words like 'many', 'several', 'countless', and so on, that seem to belong to a number system consisting of a finite (though not precisely specifiable) number of number words that 'correspond' to our numbers together with the word 'many' or 'several'.

(2) To ascertain whether two groups of things are equal in number, one need not count them: one can coordinate them either physically or notionally and so observe whether or not they are. But here, likewise, one uses two number systems: (i) one–many for without this, I should correlate many things with *one* and *one* with many. (ii) Equal–more–less (in number) which determines the final result (whether the groups are equal or not). One can imagine a language containing these systems without anyone having thought of the number series. This linguistic tool is the product of a special and tacit convention.

(3) As to the plural in relation to the two term system 1–many, this is similar to the relation between substantive and adjective: we can imagine them fused so that instead of 'bad book', 'small book', and so on we have a kind of declension, the endings doing the job of the adjectives. (Such instances do occur in Italian.) But it is much more convenient to have an independent adjective that can always be adjoined (for otherwise each substantive would need an enormous number of 'cases'). Similarly with our plural, which means 'many X'; its significance from the point of view of semantic grammar is thus that of the system '1–many'.

(4) It is senseless to ask for the essence of number as such, as for that of 'before' and 'after' as such, East and West as such and so on. If we ask an engineer about the essence of a screw he answers by showing us its function in a machine which would work differently without it, and the like. Grammar too answers questions in this way. We wonder at numbers being applicable to objects, activities and systems of every kind: six tables, six steps, six kinds, six numbers and so on. Moreover, we wonder at the fact that the number series has a beginning but no end.

We thus wonder at the specially agreed conventions and suspect them of concealing a mystery. (In particular, it is the systems whose constitution does not involve sense perception that provoke wonderment: their elements cannot be ostensively explained, hence their mysterious effect.) Clarification consists in looking at the position of number words in our language from various angles.

(5) Often we are disturbed by questions like 'what is number?', 'what is quality?' and so on. Although we really know the answer, it is as though we wished to become acquainted with the *essence* of number, quality and so on. This unease is justifiable. It does indeed make sense to ask 'what are numbers?' but it should be put thus: 'under what circumstances are number signs used? What are the rules of use? What distinguishes this whole system from others that occur in the language? What distinguishes the system's elements from each other? How does one observe these differences? How are such observations formulated correctly?' and the like.

(6) Numbers are neither proper nor general names, neither properties nor activities. These and similar negative observations belong to the meaning of number; for they tell us that number does not belong to this or that group of signs.

14. THE VERB

(1) What we call verbs in our grammar comprises several kinds of sign: for activities, processes, feelings and so on, which belong together only insofar as they all vary their form according to the tense system; more correctly, insofar as they occur merged with the tense system. The essential point is the intervention of time, rather than that of activity, which is too narrow in scope.

(2) Language is adapted mainly for describing events and not for ordering things. Hence the dominant role of the verb in sentence formation. Substantives remain untouched by time, it is grammatically inadmissible to import things into a temporal system. But one could imagine a language in which things are so defined that they take account of time. In such a language these parts of speech would have a different grammar and translation into our language would be correspondingly more difficult. (That we can successfully translate from one type of language into the other rests on the fact that the human condition does have

certain pervasive similarities. If the motives were indeed radically different, it could happen that one simply failed to understand a language, that is could not translate it.)

(3) Verbs are general names. But they can be proper names referring to unique events like X's walking this morning, or to a history that can be followed or completed continuously like X's walking as such.

(4) The tense system relates to the *whole sentence*. One could of course abolish this merger and add a tense index to the sentence, thus: 'John walking past', 'John walking future' and the like.

(5) We are dealing with a temporal system in which the point of reference must always be indicated. If I say 'I *have* played football' this means: now it belongs to the past. This 'now' is fixed by my currently speaking: it is the reference point of the three term system.

(6) The reference point may be more or less precisely fixed. If for instance we read in a diary of a polar expedition the sentence 'yesterday it was foggy and very stormy', we can range the event precisely or at least approximately. But if there is no reference point (for example if we found *only* this sentence), we must leave the question open and rest provisionally content to note that the event occurred *before* we read about it.

(7) It is wrong to believe that activities, feelings and so on are to be ranged only according to time. We may quite plausibly use place instead: 'to walk' might mean 'to walk on surface *A* near us'; 'walked', 'to walk on any surface other than *A* but not very far'; 'will walk', 'to walk on any distant surface'. Similarly, feelings and states could be 'conjugated' as to place. In such a language, the verb would no longer show time, but place. (But in this case too, the indication, though local, would refer to the whole sentence.) These and similar linguistic constructions help us above all not to cleave fanatically to the given language system.

(8) Our verb (more correctly: the sentence) is combined with temporal systems that become necessary as normal existence makes growing demands: yesterday–today–tomorrow; or if need be, the day before– after, as well as dates with or without hour, minute and so on. But these systems do not occasion novel conjugations.

(9) 'When *x* had gone, I went'. Both events belong to the past, the first being *before* the second. The past is split into 'before' and 'after'. Similarly, the future past: 'tomorrow at this hour I shall have gone';

if one takes for reference a point in the future, this event is already in the past. (If for a given moment one fixes 'front' and 'back', one can say: 'If I were standing over there, it would be at the back'.) 'Now' can be shifted into past or future and used accordingly without our leaving the present.

(10) The difference between past and past anterior may be viewed as taking a past 'present' from which the past proper is anterior. 'When I left, he had...'. This temporal situation could not be expressed if our language had no distinctions within the past, unless other words are brought in (such as 'earlier', 'later', 'already'). But if special forms are introduced, grammatical multiplicity is enhanced, a linguistic development that resembles progress in technology. Many things can be made without complex modern machinery, by those who have the various tools needed. Constructing a machine that will do the job more simply and conveniently is progress, even though craftsmen with their tools would have succeeded too.

(11) Idiom requires 'give to somebody', 'overcome somebody', 'aim at', 'strive after', 'ponder over', 'sue for', 'depend on', and so on. Beside the fact that with some verbs the relation is three term and with others two (which corresponds to the difference between indirect and direct object), the activity or state may be further defined by adding a special word. In 'strive after' the word 'after' points to the goal, as in 'run after'. Likewise for 'about' in 'worry about'. Sometimes, such usage needs to be explained by the history of philology and has nothing to do with present meanings.

(12) 'Concern oneself': the 'oneself' in such cases is not reflexive in the sense of a reflexive relation; sometimes it is rather a matter of historical reminiscence. (Certain objects have superfluous parts that are made from mere habit in the trade. Not everything about a chair can be inferred from its function; new improvements in interior design often consist merely in omitting superfluous parts.)

(13) To formulate a criterion for deciding whether a verb is reflexive or pseudo-reflexive, consider first two examples: *to behave oneself* and *to praise oneself*. We can say; *I praise myself, you, him*; but not with behave: *I behave you, I behave him* offend our sense of language. Therefore we will speak of a reflexive if we can have *xRy* as well as *xRx*. *To distress oneself* would thus seem to be a proper reflexive, for we can say to distress you, or another. However, *to distress somebody* means one or several

actions that will, as we know from experience, provoke certain reactions; whereas *to distress oneself* is a sign for a state of mind. *Oneself* in *to distress oneself* may fairly count as the mark that distinguishes this verb from the homonym meaning an action. *Oneself* is here not a variable and does not signify that we may replace it by *you* or *him*; rather, it indicates: the preceding word when referring to the same person means something else than when referring to others – *x distresses x* means a state, *x distresses y* an action. Accordingly, *I pride myself* is a peculiar formation. It looks as though it were an action, like *I wash myself*, but it should be taken as the mark of a verb of state. One can say *I make myself proud* in a reflexive sense, for here we have a verb denoting action: but not *I pride myself* in a reflexive sense. The difference further shows in that we can say *I make you proud* but not *I pride you*. Likewise, *to deceive oneself* and *to deceive somebody* differ in meaning. *I deceive myself* does not mean some special action undertaken for the purpose of deception; in contrast with the case of deceiving somebody else. We will therefore speak of a reflexive proper when it is a question of action and not state.

(14) In certain languages – such as German, French, but not Modern English – some verbs form the compound past with the auxiliary *to be*, others with *to have*, and others again with either. Such a distinction would have point only if one could state a criterion as to which auxiliary to use. For example, a verb taking *to be* might indicate a state, one taking *to have* an action; or the other way round, and the like. Such a proposal would be grammatically significant if it were wholly or largely carried through. (Since grammar is not geared to reform, we must be content simply to observe the existing chaos. In languages that lack a criterion and thus defy systematic treatment, it is therefore no wonder that the teacher of grammar is forced to treat each verb on its own.)

(15) Since indicative, subjunctive and imperative forms mark types of sentences (see III), it would be desirable for a critical grammar to use the word 'conjugation' only for mergers of activities, states and so on with the tree term tense system, or to distinguish two kinds of conjugation.

(16) The so-called finite verb is a form determined as to number, person and tense. It restricts the use of the word insofar as it can be inserted only in certain sentences that are concerned with that tense and so on. It is an instance of merged systems.

15. The various kinds of verb

(1) Let us distinguish between activities and feelings (sensations): 'I hit', 'I see'. In many languages the former type is so predominant that the latter have the same form. Hence the need to notice the difference.

(2) As to that, an activity verb may be transitive or intransitive. To the transitive form corresponds the transitive verb of feeling verbs: 'x sees y'; to intransitive activity verbs, as in 'x runs', 'x walks' and so on, evidently correspond the intransitive verbs of feeling: 'x sees, hears' and so on. Closer examination reveals the difference: intransitive feeling verbs signify that x has the disposition concerned (if colours or sounds are brought near him he behaves like one who sees or hears). 'x walks, runs' and so on also needs translating, and results in an activity (or its omission): 'x is moving his feet' and the like. To define the difference between activity and disposition, consider (i) 'A is singing', (ii) 'A can sing'. If in the morning and then that night we have observed A singing, nothing is implied as to his singing in the intervening time; but if I have observed that A *could* sing in the morning and again at night, this already expresses the sentence that he could sing in between as well. Moreover, the transitivity of feeling verbs differs from that of activity verbs: the former can be compared with events insofar as they cannot be intended, whereas the latter usually signify an intentional activity (the possibility of intention is essential to activities; see Part Two, III, 7, § 14.)

(3) Note the ambiguity of the word 'see' as feeling and activity. In the latter sense it is a transitive activity verb.

(4) Note further the difference between automatic activities and 'actions'. The latter are activities to which we relate the value system good–bad; the former are to be compared with events (process verbs) insofar as they cannot be 'valued'.

(5) Further kinds of verbs are those of state ('I am happy, sad; I rejoice' and so on) and those of process (grow, freeze and so on). The reader is invited to try his hand at formulating the grammatical difference.

16. Adverbs

(1) These comprise systems already discussed in connection with adjec-

tives, except that there they are proper or general names (class names) of objects, while here they are applied to classes of activities, feelings or states.

(2) Alongside the usual three step system of comparison for things and activities, another system is customarily applied: 'a fast runner' and 'a *very* fast runner'. 'Very' does not correspond to one of the three steps of comparison. 'A very fast runner' is neither just a fast runner (positive), nor a faster runner (comparative), nor the fastest runner (superlative), for we have here applied another system consisting of the terms 'very' and 'not so very'. (The scale of marks in a school report often contains 'good' and 'very good'.) 'Very' is not an *ad verb* but a system of degree that is combined with other systems (with adjectives of various kinds).

(3) Many other words that do not really belong here are counted as adverbs (words that do not even relate to feelings, activities, events and verbs of all kinds). Take for example 'almost'. We observe two meanings (i) where one considers a whole area but diminished by some indefinite amount. Often we are interested in the whole but do not want to omit a restriction because we are conscious of passing over a minority and intent on making this explicit. For example, 'almost the whole of Europe'; (ii) 'I was almost run over', that is it needed very little for something to have happened. The first concerns a concept, the second a sentence. As to (i), overlooking a minority is extremely important in concept formation; that is where this 'almost' belongs; in (ii), it signifies the mark of a surmise. (It is left to the reader to indicate the position of the other signs in language that are counted as adverbs.)

CHAPTER III

KINDS OF SENTENCE

1. Examples of Sentences of Various Kinds

(1) A sentence expressing a command or wish cannot at the same time be an assertion. 'I order you to do this', 'I want this to happen', are either assertions *about* ordering or wishing, or expressions of orders or wishes. (Mostly one says 'I order...' even in cases of actual orders rather than reports *about* orders. These are sentences of command that look like assertions.) Likewise, the expression 'I ask whether you are free today' is a question or an assertion, but not both at once. One cannot order that something was, is or is going to be so. For an order refers to an action that is to be carried out: something that ought to be.

If A says to B: 'take this light machine', the command sentence contains the assertion 'this machine is light'. But this sentence (like the other contained in the command, namely 'this is a machine') may be true or false and is not what is to be obeyed. Analysis here must separate assertion from command. However, the sentence 'I said (or ordered): take this light machine' does not contain a command nor a constituent that is an assertion like 'this machine is light'. (The assertion 'I said...' is not to be obeyed and remains true even if there was no machine.) This sentence requires no further dissection.

(2) In sentences of the form 'x is y' (predicative sentences, see 13) we must always observe whether we have an assertion or a sentence of grammar. For example, 'man is rational', 'man is a biped' and so on. These can explain the concept 'man' and would be correct even if some men are stupid or one-legged (for the general name means only what is typical); but in that case the corresponding universal assertions made up of the same material would be false. (If 'man' means 'most men' rather than 'all men', then even in the latter case the assertions remain true if some men are stupid or one-legged, but since they may be true or false, they still differ from the corresponding definitions.)

(3) 'To pick fruit from the tree I will put up a ladder'. This sentence

marks one activity as means, the other as end. Such sentences are called *final*. They are combinations that can be mistaken for *causal* combinations. The grammatical difference is this: in the *causal* case, an event *A* is said to be the cause of the second, *B*, the effect. If *A* is the action of a person it is still regarded as an event, irrespective of intention, whereas in the final case *A* must be an intended action. (If it is not, further analysis is required, see 5.) The causal combination cannot refer to a single event *A* as cause of *B* if it were impossible to observe any similar connection between similar events A_1 and B_1; whereas finality may well refer to individual actions.

We often speak of objects as a means or an end. This needs to be translated: the action, carried out with the help of the object, is the means or end. Means–end and cause–effect are combinations whose constituent sentences refer to events, actions and states. (Finality sometimes contains the negation of other means. In the above example we should then have to replace 'I will' by 'I must'.)

(4) The locution 'No... without...' sometimes means the empirical order of things, but may also mean the rule of usage. 'No smoke without fire', 'no son without father', 'no hill without dale'. If the former, new experience may lead one to declare such a sentence as false though hitherto regarded as true. If the latter, no experience can topple it, a rule of grammar can be displaced only if new conventions are laid down. For it is in the nature of linguistic conventions that they hold as long as they have not been replaced by others.

(5) The description of a sentence as assertion, command, wish and so on refers to what is grammatically more important, in contrast with the internal classifications of each type, which aim at grammatically subsidiary points. For the various types are then subdivided: assertions into predications, actions and so on.

(6) The question mark at the end of an interrogative sentence, like the 'if' at the beginning of a conditional, marks the type. For there are keys that characterize everything that follows (see IV), and others that apply only to single sentences. A language in which all sentence types are marked by special signs would eliminate many misunderstandings.

(7) If someone says 'it will soon get better', without indication whether this is a wish or a forecast (nor possibility of finding out by asking the speaker about the rules of usage), then trying to find out is a search for

the *sense* of the sentence; though to determine it, one has to make use of certain empirical findings. The hearer's reflections based on experience consist in surmises, assertions and so on, resulting in the observation: this is a forecast, or wish, or ambiguous between the two but certainly not a command, and so on. Such assessments often proceed so automatically that the hearer (or *we*, after having heard the sentence), asked whether he can recall these speculations, will answer with an unconditional no. Nevertheless we are entitled to describe them, because they become 'conscious' in certain cases where the point is deliberate analysis of a dubious sentence. Take, for example, reading: someone who understands English reads to us from a book; at the end of a chapter we ask him what he thinks about some sentence or other, and he replies that while reading he had been thinking about something else altogether. Still, he has performed correctly, with proper stress and pauses and all the rest, quite automatically as it were. It is only someone still *learning* the language who tends to think about how to stress this or that word correctly. Likewise as to understanding the meaning of single signs and the sense of their combinations. Only where the language machine breaks down, where the sense of certain sentences is in doubt, will we take notice of how the machine functions. Of course the man who hears 'it will soon get better' can simply refrain from grammatical analysis and verify the sentence by subsequent observations; but in that case he will have verified only the forecast, not the speaker's intention.

2. Subjunctive sentences

(1) The word 'surmise', which marks subjunctive sentences, is used in the sense of 'suppose', 'consider as true', 'provisionally assume to be true'. To ensure against a psychologistic view of the subjunctive, note that any assertion about the future, even those attended by a special feeling of certainty, are logically speaking sentences of subjunctive form. If a feeling of uncertainty were to be taken as criterion for surmises, and conviction for definite sentences, then a sentence like 'tomorrow the sun will rise' would be no surmise or conjunctive sentence but an indicative one.

(2) Let us call indicative those sentences that we or other people whom we trust have already verified beyond doubt; and subjunctive those that

we merely assume pending verification. (This, too, is meant by the usual distinction between the modal forms of the verb, which exhibit a difference between *two sentence types*. The two forms attaching to the verb mislead us to believe that it is a special concern of the verb.)

(3) Subjunctive and indicative varies from person to person: what is certain for *A* may be merely assumed by *B* or conversely.

(4) Both provisional surmise and conviction, subjunctive and indicative, are keys marking a sentence as to verification. The subjunctive sentence: 'I believe...' expresses a true statement only pending verification; this combination of words loses its function when conviction supervenes. The indicative sentence, however, expresses a true sentence at the moment of speaking.

(5) What motivates formation of subjunctive sentences is the fact that one was often unable to verify an assertion in the usual way and could verify it only partly. One was thus content to assert it as a surmise, which expresses the expectation that it would yet turn out true. Later, surmises as a type came to shed the tie to subsequent verification. This holds for example for the form 'suppose that *p*...'. This assumption differs from the usual one in that it is a *combination* of sentences, and can be true even when *p* is false.

(6) The difference between indicative and subjunctive refers *only* to assertions, but not to questions, commands and wishes. Likewise, a convention of logic cannot appear in subjunctive form. Questions, commands and rules are logically inadmissable as surmises (or possibilities).

3. Causal Sentences

(1) The individual causal sentence ('because...') presupposes a general causal sentence ('if...') and a conclusion, it signifies the application of the general proposition to the particular case. For example: 'this plant is green, therefore it is pleasing to my eyes'. It contains the general causal sentence 'green objects are pleasant to the eyes' and the conclusion 'this object is green, therefore it is pleasant to my eyes'.

(2) The individual causal sentence, the 'because' sentence, speaks of the order of things in a singular way, and must not be confused with the general 'if' sentence, for it describes the observed order events *as such*; but in the 'because' sentence this order is presupposed.

(3) A sentence whose second part begins with 'for', 'because', 'therefore' is thus marked as complex and not a function of its parts: the whole sentence need not be true even if both parts are. For example 'X is going home because he is tired' analyses into (i) 'X is going home'; (ii) 'X is tired'; (iii) '(ii) is the cause of (i)'. The 'because' sentence contains (i) and (ii), without them it would be absurd; but its truth requires more than their joint truth.

(4) This holds for the individual causal sentence; the general 'if' sentence however, for example 'if bodies are released, they fall to the ground', is not to be dissected into 'bodies have been released', 'they have fallen to the ground' and a separate 'because' sentence. On the contrary, from the 'if' sentence one can derive an infinite series of 'if' and 'because' sentences: 'if at such and such a time and place I release a body, then...'; 'this body has fallen to the ground because...'

(5) The causal 'if' is not to be confused with that conditional 'if' which may be regarded as the logical key for the relation of ground and consequence. In 'if all men are mortal and Socrates is a man, then...' the first part can be transformed into an independent unconditional sentence 'all men are mortal', from which the second part 'Socrates is mortal' can be inferred. But this holds only for 'if' sentences expressing the relation of ground and consequence, not for the causal 'if' sentences. This may serve as criterion for the difference.

(6) Unfortunately, language often uses the same material for both causal and conditional sentences, although one perceives the beginnings of a distinction (especially in singular sentences): 'therefore' tends to be used mainly for ground and consequence, more clearly still with 'consequently' and the like.

4. Notes on end, cause, ground, and motive

(1) These words are grammatical terms insofar as they characterize certain sentence types that share certain features: they consist of parts but are nevertheless to be verified independently. But there are grammatical differences; that between end on the one hand and cause or ground on the other seems obvious, we find it even at a more primitive level. But that between end on the one hand and ground or motive on the other arises from somewhat more complex grammatical reflection.

(2) As to the concept of purpose: the expression 'means without end' is grammatically barred, just as 'cause without effect'. Compare this with the combination of sentences 'if..., then...'. Forming an absolute condition or 'if' sentence consisting only of the first part seems absurd.

Hence we should equally resist pronouncing a conditional sentence of the form 'if p, then p', Likewise there is a bar on calling p both means and purpose (or cause and effect). The phrase 'it is both means and end' is logically barred unless read as follows: A is a means to the end B; but within B in turn, one can distinguish between means and end, so that B_1 may be called both means and end, namely means to B_2 and end of A. If a savage grabs a stone to crack a nut, then the stone (or rather, the acts performed with it) is means to the end of nutcracking. But if he works the stone to give purchase to the thumb and a close fit to the hollow hand to facilitate grabbing, then the finished stone is the end. Hence we may say that the worked stone is both means and end. A glimpse at a workshop is enough to visualize how widely this system may be applied.

The expression 'absolute end', like 'absolute cause' is misleading, since what makes the means–end system usable is that it can be shifted and variously applied. For example, if we always described eating as an end and all preparatory work as means, they would be general names for eating and preparation, and not a means–end system. Likewise for 'absolute cause'.

(3) To bring out more sharply the difference between cause on the one hand and ground and motive on the other, consider some examples. (a) 'x is smaller than y $(=p)$, hence y is greater than x $(=q)$'; (b) 'the snow in the mountains has melted $(=p)$, hence the rivers are in spate $(=q)$'. (a) is a case of ground and consequence, (b) of cause and effect. In (a), p can be grammatically transformed into q, in (b) not. That is, in (a) p cannot be true or false without q being so, whereas in (b) p can be true and q false or conversely. If one becomes aware of the different 'hence' in the two cases, one will have learnt to keep cause and ground apart. (To retain the difference and to explain it to oneself and others, one uses brief formulations or lengthy examples that seem appropriate to making such differences plausible. Each method has advantages and drawbacks; it is therefore *advisable* to try both.)

(4) If a judge asks the accused why he has committed the punishable

offence, this is not a request for a cause but for the motive for the resolution to act; the psychiatrist brought into the proceedings seeks mainly for the cause of the deed.

(5) Assume a graphologist had unambiguous criteria for distinguishing the handwriting of intelligent persons from that of less intelligent ones, and suppose that the use of printed letters indicates the more intelligent hand. Suppose further that someone who partly writes in printed characters has read about this criterion in a book on graphology, and, being ambitious, he now tries to make his writing still more like printing. We can then say that until he read the book his handwriting was a significant symptom, because it could be regarded only in causal terms; but since reading it, the causal nexus is disturbed by a motive which now becomes a cause.

(6) With regard to any 'valued' action we shall speak of a motive, and of a ground with regard to logical situations. A motive presupposes a special resolution of the will, a consequence merely a general adherence to the rules of the language.

5. INTERROGATIVE SENTENCES

(1) These derive from the need to learn any fact, the end being to replace doubt or partial knowledge that do not issue in definite modes of behaviour in practical life, by an assertion that enables us to find our way completely: the answer.

(2) Most questions presuppose certain facts as known, that is, their analysis shows certain assertions. Sometimes the question refers to the unknown ground (end, motive) or the unknown cause of known facts and so on. According to what is unknown, we distinguish various kinds of question. Since everything can be questioned, there are as many types of question as of assertion. (We leave the reader to ponder whether *every* question presupposes some knowledge, so that its analysis contains an assertion.)

(3) The word 'question' marks a certain kind of sentence and is thus distinguished from other sentences. The observation of the difference leads us to form the word. We can make this difference more precise in various ways, of which we note only one: if we link an ordinary sentence with its negative by 'or' we obtain an uninformative combination or

tautology, for example 'the sun is shining or the sun is not shining'; not so with questions, where 'is the sun shining or is it not shining?' is the very paradigm of a precise question. (What is common to questions and assertions is that combining positive with negative by 'and' yields nonsense in both cases.)

The word 'question' (or 'ask') is a grammatical concept and arose through grammatical specialization. It belongs to the observation of differences between sentence types.

(4) Questions refer *only* to assertions, not to commands or wishes. *A* commands: bring me that book. *B* asks: which? His question refers to greater definition of a concept in the command, but by first changing it into an assertion to which the question refers: you ask me to bring you a book, which book do you mean? Asking after a command refers to the assertion that the command was or will be issued, or to the presuppositions behind the command and the like. Nor can one ask after a question. Asking somebody 'did you ask?' refers to the assertion. (Do not questions like 'what is your command?' refer to the command? But in what sense?)

(5) We know questions that can be answered yes or no, where the answer is *already prepared or suggested* in the question. For example: 'Is the sun shining outside?' or 'Is this the right road sign or not?' Such questions as the related type of *disjunctive questions* of the form 'Is it *A* or *B* or *C*?' will be taken together here. The latter are indeed not answered by yes or no, but the answer is prepared.

Then there are questions not to be so answered, where an answer is provoked but not prepared, for example 'What is the name of your brother's friend?'

Questions of the first kind are usually marked by word order; and those of the second kind by certain interrogative words like 'why', 'what', 'how' and so on, usually with corresponding words in the answers, like 'because', 'that' and so on. The interrogative words are used also in cases where there is obviously no question; for example 'why did you do this' (reprovingly) or 'what beautiful scenery!' (admiringly), where tone or exclamation mark point to a different mode of use and indicate the sentence type.

(6) 'Whether' in a sentence about the question marks the latter as requiring yes or no as an answer, or as a disjunctive question of several

members (whether *a* or *b* or *c*). 'Why' refers to sentences of cause, ground or motive; (the grammar of these questions thus presupposes a grammar for those types, together with the general interrogative rules. Since all questions share these last, the terms 'question' and 'interrogative sentence' seem justified).

(7) The interrogative words 'what', 'whose', 'whom' show us where to look for the question in the assertion. (i) What have you here? (ii) What has he done? (iii) What did I think? The first presupposes the sentence 'You (already a proper name) have something here'. The question refers to the name of the object. Likewise in (ii), but with the range of reply referring to actions, whereas it is confined to things in (i) and to thoughts (sentences) in (iii).

(8) 'Whose' refers to the genitive, 'whom' to the accusative and 'to whom' to the dative. Questions with those keys refer to relational sentences and may be expressed in relational symbols. 'Whose house is this' = '$R(a, x)$?' Likewise 'To whom will you give the book?' = '$R(a, x, b)$?', or 'What book will you give John ?' = '$R(a, b, x)$?', where the three letters stand for giver, receiver and gift respectively. (For 'R' see 12).

(9) 'Which town was it?' Here 'which' asks after the proper name, but it can refer also to general names. 'Which kind of' introduces questions as to making general names more precise. 'Who' and 'where' serve to mark a type of question as well as to introduce the sign of a proper name (a case of economy.)

(10) *A* to *B*: 'Can you tell me...?' This question literally refers to the disposition or ability of *B*. If *A* wishes to ascertain the facts as such, the formula 'can you' though common, is most inadequate. For it signifies that he merely wishes to find out whether *B* knows this or that; a situation in which 'can you tell me...?', 'do you know if...?', and the like are adequate ways of starting the question, while the usual form of question 'where does *X* live' and so on is inadequate. Often the question aims at the other person's opinion rather than at the facts ('will it rain', 'will it end well?', and the like). One is in the process of testing a sentence and therefore collects views and convictions and decides afterwards. These are like voting slips that are counted to decide who will represent the people.

(11) A counter-question, if on analysis it contains a reply, is to be taken as an answer to the question.

(12) Questions are in a certain sense commands of a specific kind, inviting linguistic actions. (While other commands relate to all kinds of actions, questions are directed to specific actions such as thinking, speaking, writing and so on.)

(13) Amongst the subdivisions of interrogative sentences are those as to time, place, end, cause, ground, number, measure and so on. For all these, the prior questions as to events, states and so on are to be answered yes or no or at best surmised.

(14) Interrogatives of place 'where', 'whence', 'whither', if not metaphorical (whence = ancestry, whither = end, and the like) form a three term system. To grasp the motive for this, imagine a man going from A to B and now at some point U which is the reference point of the system answering to 'where?', while 'whence' and 'whither' refer to starting point and goal respectively.

(15) A: 'Where does X live?'; B: 'I do not know', that is, I am unacquainted with the assertion that answers the question; or B: 'I do not know X', for asking presupposes knowing, so that one may answer by pleading ignorance of the assertion presupposed in the question.

(16) Questions as to place 'where', 'whence', 'whither', 'how far' refer not only to a metric or measure applied to the place; they may be answered also by means of words belonging to vague systems, indeed quite often by very vague indications such as 'not far', 'very far' and the like.

(17) Questions as to time 'when', 'at what time', 'since when', 'till when' can be answered 'early', 'till later' and so on, or metrically 'at 5 o'clock', 'since last year', 'in a week's time' and so on.

(18) A question as to end often begins with 'for what purpose' and refers to actions. After repeated questions as to the end of such actions one reaches a state that is be produced. Questions as to end can be asked in different senses. If I ask someone for example 'why did you tie your shoelaces this morning?' we note first that the question cannot really be asked, since one can ask for the end only where the action is not automatic or customary but follows a decision of the will. The question refers to a mode of behaviour that can be viewed as a purposive action. The answer would have to be taken in the same way: 'had I considered the matter I should have done it to this end'. (Explain questions of this kind as regards a whole cultural setting: 'why are shoes worn?' and the like.)

(19) A question as to end shares with one as to cause (or time and so on) a prior question whose answer is presupposed. If I ask 'why, for what purpose, when did you do this?' I must first settle the prior question 'did you do this?'

(20) 'Why', 'for what reason' and so on are questions as to cause or ground (or motive). The signs for ground and cause are often the same, which shows a lack of grammatical reflection.

(21) Questions as to number 'how many is that?' are ambiguous as to cardinal or ordinal.

6. DOUBT

(1) This, too, relates to assertions. The difference between question and doubt consists in that the former contains an invitation that initiates a linguistic action aiming at the stationary state of an answer, while the latter lacks this imperative impulse. Doubt is usually as to truth or falsehood of a sentence (or the following or disobeying of a command) and takes the form: 'matters stand thus or thus, I do not know' ('should I do it or not, I do not know'). This resembles the case of those questions in which the answer is prepared. Doubt may take also the form 'p or q or r, I do not know'. But one can doubt only if a given number of sentences are before us. (What is doubt concerning a sentence of grammar?)

(2) Because of the element 'I do not know' we cannot doubt things we do know, but one can ask even when one knows (namely to test others).

(3) Questions are in the first instance peculiar to dialogue, while doubt belongs to monologue.

(4) Just as questions must be separated from reproaches in that grammatically the former requires an answer while the latter does not, so doubt must be distinguished from the asserted alternative. The sentence, 'my father or my uncle is in the room' becomes doubt only when it relates to a dicision yet to be made.

(5) The element of ignorance clearly presupposes a system of language that contains the difference T–F. Doubts such as 'are there true sentences or not?' are barred because they employ language that presupposes the grammar of T–F. If a sceptic points to error and deception in order to deny truth, we point out to him that error and deception too presuppose this grammar. (The sentence 'there is no truth' can mean only 'let us leave the language form of assertions, questions and assumptions';

for as soon as someone asserts or asks anything, he uses a form of language that presupposes the difference $T-F$.)

7. COMMANDS

(1) These are in the first place to be taken as between people: A orders B to do something. Regarded as a relation, commanding has three terms. 'Intention' is a command of the form 'A orders A', as when someone intends to do something. If he fails to do it, the sentence is not a false forecast but a disobeying of the command (intention).

(2) Commands relate to future actions, *not to facts or the past*. But it may relate to refraining from action ('do not stop!') to directing attention ('beware of trains!') to acquiring dispositions ('understand this sentence!') and the like. A command has sense if it can be followed, that is if the assertion describing its being followed has sense.

(3) A command usually aims at a goal that both or at least the commander can indicate. Often a command is 'founded' on this goal: 'bring me the boards, because I want to build a hut' (see § 16). (The goal of the goal and so on are presupposed as obvious.) In general commands, as in law or custom, it can happen that we no longer know the goal, particularly since we can at best conjecture as to the legislators and their aims; although they did have them.

(4) Word combinations like 'to command to stones', 'hark ye mountains!' are barred insofar as it belongs to the rules for using the concepts 'stone' and 'mountain' that they neither obey nor disobey: one can command only where orders are followed or not. For although it is only a matter of experience that mountains and certain animals do not react to command, it is precisely these experiences that have led to grammatical 'parts of speech' that are linked with logical vetoes. If our language admitted those sentences, then we should have to describe non-reaction to commands as stones or mountains disobeying orders. (The borderline between organisms that can be commanded and those where we cannot speak of orders is vague, though it is clear that we can give orders to a dog but not to a snail.)

(5) A command can relate only to what is logically possible. One can indeed order someone to travel to the planets but not to London yesterday.

(6) One can compare commands with logical rules which relate to

linguistic actions and hold until repealed. But logical rules relate to signs and thereby differ from general commands. (See above, the difference between convention and observation: the latter is an historical statement as to how people use certain concepts in certain fields, the former is normative. A linguistic observation has this in common with conventions, that they are its object: one observes that a convention has been adopted and obeyed.)

(7) We distinguish singular and general commands: that a singular command has been followed can be ascertained from a *single* case, like the truth of a single assertion; but the assertion describing that a general command has been obeyed always contains the words 'until now'.

(8) If we compare this with linguistic conventions we find a difference in that they *can never be quite singular*. They may indeed be confined to one field or period but not to a *unique* instance of naming; whereas commands (other than political or moral laws) relate to *unique* actions.

(9) Linguistic conventions are instructions for use. If they are of the form 'by *x* I will understand such and such', the assertion of the will concerns only the initial decision; the implicit intention to abide by it amounts to a command: the author gives an order to himself. The other form of convention; '*x* shall mean such and such', corresponds to ordinary commands issued to others.

(10) Every intention of an individual, every custom, social convention or law of the community, is a command. If members of a community are asked about the laying down of the law and they all agree, then the laws hold in virtue of the intention of each member (*A* gives orders to *A*). In such cases it is usually the majority that decides (*A* gives orders to *B*, where *A* is the majority and *B* the opponents of the law).

(11) An example of a mode of expression that signifies both intention and command: 'well then, let us...'. It is a command addressed both to oneself and to others.

(12) Commands are invitations to do something. But are speeches like 'I invite (or command) you to do such and such' commands or assertions? To this there is no general answer, for it depends on the tone in which they are spoken, on the circumstances of their utterance and so on. Often 'I command you to...' amounts to 'do such and such'. (Note that awareness of the difference between command and an assertion about commanding arises only at an advanced level of grammatical

differentiation. One can compare it with the difference between 'here *is* a tree' and 'here I *see* a tree': it requires special grammatical reflection to grasp that the second can be true without the first being so).

(13) What of commands where the commander is not too serious about obedience? Or statements that are written up and the writer never thought of them as commands, but others merely misconstrued them as such? The answer is that a command, like any sentence, is not a sentence 'in itself'. It is a sentence insofar as someone regards it as such, and like-wise a command; that is, insofar as it is assigned a certain position within language. Thus for the writer it might not be a command, yet for the reader it might. For the commander it can be a command only insofar as the others react to it accordingly. All these commands share with genuine commands that *everybody* locates correctly a common 'intersection of meaning', which accounts for their sharing the name.

The following example shows the importance of how sentences are understood. Some time ago I saw two faces of a clock at a street corner, showing 2.15 and 2.30 respectively. For me as reader of the two sentences they contain a contradiction: the number system and time reckoning is the same but one face shows 2.15 and the other 2.30. But it would be senseless to say that the clock 'in itself' was contradictory. Another example: it can happen that signs on antique vessels are misconstrued as writing, even to the point of discovery of what is inscribed. What here appears as a word is then a word insofar as we give it meaning. But the sentence that the maker had put inscriptions on the vessels is false. The reverse may happen: a genuine script may appear to be mere ornament, so that for the author it consists of words, but for us of meaningless strokes, so long as we do not discover their meaning.

(14) 'John!' 'Look!' 'Listen!' 'Quiet!' 'Come here!' and the like all have the form of commands and relate to another's future activities (or their cessation) directed at a certain goal. (The exclamation mark belongs to the key of these sentences; but it is neither necessary nor sufficient to mark a command.) Although one of our examples is a proper name, it is meant in the sense of a command, signifying according to circumstances 'come here!', 'Listen!' and so on. Commands as to seeing and hearing are meant to direct the attention, the turning of eyes or ears or head, but not seeing and hearing as such. One can order someone to do something but not to sense something. (This observation also

applies in Part Two, II, 15). The seeing in the command 'see here!' is not like the seeing in 'I see such and such'; it is meant in the sense of 'look', just as 'hear' is in the sense of 'listen'. In using the word 'quiet!' one evidently means refraining from speech or noises rather than the word as such, for a concept cannot be a command.

(15) Commands relating to omissions may be called negative. If the positive sentence is followed, the corresponding negative one is disobeyed and conversely. Commands joined to their negatives by 'and' ('go away and do not go away!') offend against the rules just as the corresponding assertions. But joining a command with its negative by 'or' robs it of its imperative character, (with assertions, this corresponds to tautology). 'Go away or do not go away!' provokes no action, for it is always 'obeyed'. We need not first observe whether B has gone out or not to ascertain whether he has acted according to the command, for his action 'necessarily' conforms to it.

(16) A command cannot at the same time be a cause or ground. If someone is told 'go away, because the air is stale here', the part introduced by 'because' is not a command; 'because' here relates to the assertion 'I order you to go away'. A command cannot be founded, only the sentence *that* somebody is commanding can.

(17) Commands can be tied to conditions relating to the circumstances under which they are to be followed. ('If there is no rain, fetch water for the animals!') A command itself cannot be split into an if-clause and a then-clause.

(18) Consider this problem: a teacher explaining certain scientific expressions to his pupils might tell them: 'By mass we are to understand such and such'. What is the function of such sentences? Are they *conventions*? Not at first blush, for the teacher has not laid them down. *Observations*? No, indeed. Did he wish to indicate merely the usage of the word in a certain period? For evidently he requests that his pupils *should* use the word in that sense. What, then, is it? For clarification, let us look at another example. Consider how orders are given in the field: from general staff to officers to men. The element of comparison of interest here is the command given by the officers. In a certain sense it is no longer a command in its original meaning, insofar as it involves no decision or desired result. This side of commands is missing in the orders given by officers, but in its effect on the soldiers it is to be described as a

command because it causes the men to act. Likewise with the 'conventions' laid down by the teacher.

8. WISHES

(1) To mark a sentence as a wish, one has to consider whether it can be fulfilled. For a wish cannot be true or false, nor can it be answered, nor followed, but it can be realized.

(2) A wish is not issued to someone. As a relation, wishing has not, like commanding, three terms but only two: X wishes Y, where X stands only for living creatures and Y *not* for objects. ('I wish you such and such' means that I wish that a certain state should supervene.)

(3) Wishes relate to the occurrence of future events and states. An optative sentence has sense if the assertion describing the desired state has sense.

(4) A wish cannot be founded, only the sentence *that* someone wishes can (see commands).

(5) One way of marking the difference between wish and command is to observe that commands provoke action towards a certain state conceived as goal by the commander, while wishes do not provoke such action: nor is the desired state the goal of an action, but the content of the wish.

(6) If I wish that today (a weekday) be Sunday, what I desire (given that I accept our current system of weeks and months) is peace and the sort of outing usual on Sundays, not what is logically imposssible. I cannot wish to be alive and dead at once. (What of the wish to be a spectator at one's own demise and afterwards? Does this mean no more than if someone after an operation looks at a severed portion of his own body?)

9. ADVICE

(1) A asks B for advice and B replies 'do such and such!' or 'it is well if you do that!' Advice can be tendered in several forms: as command or assertion. (Request, advice and question are related in that they occasion another's actions. Hence they can be contrasted as a group with the group of assertion, doubt and wish.)

(2) An honest and well-considered piece of advice involves B putting himself in A's situation, asking himself how he would act under these

circumstances and weighing the assertion, namely 'were I to find myself in such a position, I should do such and such'. But this is not a surmise: for if *B* did later so find himself without thus acting, one could still not say that his advice was false. For insofar as he has weighed up the relevant motives and reached a certain conclusion which he then imparted to *A*, his sentence is to be taken as 'genuine' advice that is independent of his own actions.

(3) We distinguish genuine from sham advice, according to the adviser's honesty and motive.

(4) Sayings are partly general advice valid for a certain series of cases. (But they also relate to the order of experienced occurrences and are to be regarded as vague laws of events insofar as they enable one to predict. By means of this causal element they may also be stated as general conditionals.)

10. NEGATIVE SENTENCES

(1) Negation relates to sentences. 'Negative concepts' consist of a sign (an element of any system) and the negation sign, so that if they occur in a certain way in a sentence, the positive sentence can be translated into a negative one. An example will make this clear: a builder can arrange his bricks in such a way as to dress some of them with mortar or cement, so that whenever he needs one such he spares himself the trouble of dressing each individually. That is the function of 'negative concepts'.

(2) In symbolic logic, 'classes' (corresponding to general names discussed above) are denoted by Greek letters α, β, γ and so on, and the negative classes by $-\alpha$, $-\beta$, $-\gamma$. But such concept formation has sense only with regard to a certain domain of proper or general names that is split into α and $-\alpha$. But if no domain is envisaged, no negative classes can be formed. The expression 'non-table' can be formed only where one has first envisaged for instance the class of pieces of furniture and then wants to exclude a part of it (benches, chairs, beds and so on). This part is now given a name and that is the 'negative class'.

(3) We distinguish systems of signs in which the direction (positive or negative) has been fixed for the whole language, and others that were formed by means of negation but without preferred direction. To these

atter belong those pairs of words that can be described as mutual
[1]negatives, such as: courageous–cowardly, rest–motion, reveal–conceal
and the like, without marking the direction of negation. They imply
that sentences respectively containing them are incompatible, so that
one sentence is denoted as negation with regard to the other. Substi-
tuting the 'opposite element' changes the sense of the sentence, but it
remains as before, neither positive nor negative.

(4) Usually the positive sentence is regarded as *the* sentence and the
negative one its negation. But we could equally well take the negative
sentences as basic and regard the positive ones as requiring special
explanation.

(5) To observe grammatically whether a system consisting let us say
of a and b contains no further elements, put the signs (a, b) into sentences
of the form 'x is a or b', where the decision as to substitution for x is
left to one's logically trained sense of language: if the sentence so formed
is 'obviously true' without the need for verifying it by means of empirical
data, then a and b form a 'closed system', where a is to be denoted as the
negative of b and b of a; but if this is not so, then a and b belong either to
different systems or to one system that has additional members or that
at present is still (or already) fragmentrary (systems of concepts often
confront us in the course of growth or atrophy, as is seen retrospectively
if later they grow or wither further) or there is a region of vagueness
between a and b.

(6) A system which has no further elements is called closed. This
shows itself in that a sentence like 'x is large or small' is always true, so
long as the two adjectives fit x and the region of vagueness is left out of
account (so that small=not large and large=not small); but 'x is white
or blue' can be false even when x is coloured. That is the difference
between 'contradictory' and 'contrary' in classical logic. For two concepts
that form a closed system, sentences that contain them are subject to
the rule that the truth of the one statement follows from the falsehood
of the contradictory opposite and conversely. But if the system consists
of many members, the rule is that from the truth of one statement follows
the falsehood of every contrary, and from the falsehood of one the truth
of the disjunction of all its contraries. (If 'the table is red' is false, this
means that 'the table is yellow or green or...' is true.) The schema for
contradictories is

$$
\begin{array}{ll}
p \quad \bar{p} \quad (=\text{not-}p) & T = \text{true} \\
T \quad F & F = \text{false} \\
F \quad T &
\end{array}
$$

The schema for contraries of a closed system of three terms is

$$
\begin{array}{lll}
p & q & r \\
T & F & F \\
F & T & F \\
F & F & T
\end{array}
$$
This schema which can have any number of terms will be called the 'contrary schema'.

(7) 'Not bad' is not the same as 'good', nor 'not little' the same as 'much'. Although good–bad and little–much are closed systems without further terms, nevertheless the terms of these systems are not sharply marked off from each other: between them lies a 'region of vagueness' so that the negation of one term is not identical with the other. In saying that such systems follow the rule for contradictories, we have left the intervening region of vagueness out of account.

(8) Negation is not a combination of sentences as produced by 'and', 'or', 'if–then' and so on (see Part Two, IV, 2). However, it does not relate to concepts but to sentences, hence we use the symbols for sentences p, q, r and not the signs for concepts variables x, y, z. (To give due emphasis to the grammatically important difference between concept and sentence one uses different symbols.)

(9) Our negation relates to all kinds of sentences: assertions, questions, commands and so on. But notice that its function differs for the different types: a question cannot be denied in the same sense as an assertion. Denying an assertion is asserting its contradictory, while a 'negative question' is negative only insofar as it presupposes (or contains) a negative sentence. 'Why are you not going?' presupposes that the other is not going. But one cannot ask negatively, for as a question the sentence is precisely neither positive nor negative. (A command is called negative if following it is to be represented by a negative sentence.)

(10) Traditional logic distinguishes universal and particular propositions depending on whether all or only one or some members of a domain are covered; this is then combined with the distinction between positive and negative. As to that we note that *every* sentence can be negated, including those where no distinction between universal and particular

applies, as for example in reports of sensations: 'I hear a sound' and so on. The difference positive–negative may however be combined with the difference assertion–command–question. Indeed that is where such a schema would be worthwhile. *For although the negation of commands or questions resembles the negation of assertions, it is nevertheless different.* (The reader is invited to formulate this difference precisely!)

11. EXISTENTIAL SENTENCES

(1) In our language there occur sentences like: 'there are negative numbers', 'there are pygmies', 'there is a moon', "there is a word 'and'" and so on. Since existential sentences differ amongst themselves, it is first necessary to point to the differences.

(2) An example will explain this: a teacher wo wishes to ascertain whether his pupils have understood the words 'negative numbers' (A), 'pygmies' (B), 'moon' (C) and 'and' (D), asks them various questions: where are $ABCD$? (in the sense of place). When are $ABCD$? Can one see, hear, feel them? If the pupils are clear about this, they will above all answer taking A and D (and B and C) together. Irrespective of the truth or falsehood of their answers, they would give place and time with B and C, and other systems with A and D, since for the latter place and time offend against the rules. If a pupil said for example that negative numbers are in his textbook or on the blackboard the teacher used yesterday or today, the answer would be wrong. It would be equally wrong if he answers C by citing the moon's picture in the textbook, with this difference: the system remains the same insofar as both moon and moon picture are localisable and visible. The error is thus slighter, whereas with A and D there is a logical misunderstanding: misconstruing the material as carrying the meaning. (We leave the reader to try to formulate the difference between the two errors grammatically.) The question 'when' with regard to A and D is against the rules too, for in the answer 'in the mathematics or language that certain people have used at a certain period', the time indication refers to *use* and not to A and D themselves. The questions as to sense perception must also be answered in different ways: with A and D one can see only the material of the sign, if written; hear it, if spoken; feel it, if represented in relief, for example. It is senseless to speak of perceiving what is designated, one can only understand it.

But with *B* and *C* one can perceive what is designated in ways similar to perceiving the material of the signs. (This requires further elucidation. See the explanations on cross-sections.)

(3) If an existential sentence relates to objects (like *B* and *C*), we distinguish two types: (i) an existential sentence in which a spatio-temporally bounded domain is indicated as for example 'there are pygmies in Africa at present'. If we have travelled throughout Africa and found that there were none, then the sentence is false. (ii) an existential sentence without such a domain being indicated, for example 'there are (were, will be) pygmies'. This is not fasified by examining a given area to see whether such a race does live there. But here too it must be possible to indicate a method for determining truth *or* falsehood. (The sentence 'there will never be centaurs' is significant because if any centaur were ever found, the sentence would have been falsified.)

(4) The following analogy throws light on the first kind of existential sentence: someone walking on a path felt as though near a given place he had lost a coin. Looking in the relevant places he either finds the coin or infers that he had lost none. If the former then the sentence 'near this place there might be a lost coin of mine' becomes superfluous; if the latter, that sentence becomes false.

(5) For sentences like those about *A* and *D* (where spatio-temporal and sense perception data are grammatically inadmissible) an analogous difference holds insofar as they can mean two things: (i) 'there is a word 'and' within such and such a system of signs', and (ii) 'there is a word 'and' within some system of signs'.

12. RELATIONS

(1) The theory of relations worked out by Russell is an important part of the grammar of certain signs in our language, such as 'to the right of' 'earlier', 'father', 'smaller' and so on. Sentences formed with them are called relational sentences. A few observations on this theory and its terms may be made by way of examples. The following sentences, quoted as examples, are rules or conventions as to certain words: a relation is called *reflexive* if it can hold between *A* and *A*, irreflexive if not; thus the meaning of words like 'to love' is laid down in such a way that one can say '*A* loves *A* (himself)'; words like 'left', 'father' (and also the

word 'similar' in ordinary language) may not be so used: sentences like '*A* to the left of *A*' are inadmissible.

'A relation is called *symmetrical* if it holds between *A* and *B* and between *B* and *A*'. This is not here meant as an assertion of applied language but a grammatical observation concerning the use of words like 'as big as', 'different from each other' and so on. It is to express the veto on forming sentences like '*A* is as big as *B* but *B* is not as big as *A*'. For it belongs to the definition of these words that they can be used only symmetrically whereas words like 'bigger' must not be used symmetrically (so called logical symmetry).

'A relation is called *transitive* if its holding between *A* and *B*, and *B* and *C*, entails its holding between *A* and *C*'. That is, it belongs to the grammar of certain words like 'earlier' that if *A* is earlier than *B* and *B* than *C*, then one cannot say that *A* is not earlier than *C*. With other words such as for example 'father' transitivity is barred. One must not say '*A* is father of *B*, and *B* of *C*, and also *A* of *C*'.

(2) Insofar as the terms *a* and *b* in '*a* loves *b*' and in '*a* greater than *b*' may for instance not be inverted without altering the sense of the sentence or insofar as both differ from '*a* is walking', it seems justified to represent them in symbols as $x R y$ (R=relation). Nevertheless, the two sentences are grammatically different. If R stands for 'to love', the place of x in $x R y$ can be taken only by living creatures, whereas if R is 'greater than', we may substitute also 'street'. But where substitutions differ in this way, the symbolism must not deceive us as to their presence.

(3) One could for example further introduce $x A y$, $x S y$ (A=activity, S=sensation) and the like; for activities and sensations differ as to grammar from other relations such as kinship relations (x is the father of y) and the like: if one writes $x R y$ this already entitles one to write $y R x$, producing another sentence with the same elements. Putting 'John' for x, 'axe' for y, 'raise' for R, $x R y$ means 'John is raising the axe'. But we cannot say 'the axe is raising John', for in that sentence 'raise' would mean something else (with '$x A y$', we must bar '$y A x$' if A stands for certain activities). If x is the cousing of y, $x R y$, then y can be the cousin of z, $y R z$; but if y is inanimate we cannot form $y A z$ although $x A y$ does obtain.

(4) Other differences appear if for R we put sensations as in 'x sees y' where 'see' is not meant in the sense of looking; hence our previous

suggestion to represent these as $x\ S\ y$. 'S' can be reflexive, if suitably interpreted. (These hints are to induce the reader to formulate and perhaps symbolize the differences between relations.)

(5) The words 'earlier' and 'greater' have much in common: both presuppose two terms of comparison and belong to domains with gradations. The domains can be bounded to mark a lowest and highest degree (positive and superlative), but they may be indefinitely continued at both ends. (All this forms the 'intersection' of the grammatical terms 'time' and 'magnitude'.) The words 'earlier' and 'greater' have common rules: if a is before b, then not b before a; if a is greater than b, then not b greater than a. Both divide the domain into two parts, both have a converse (later, smaller). The concept 'father' shows many similarities with these; the grammatical concept 'ancestry' has a common intersection with the concepts 'time', 'magnitude', 'multiplicity, and so on. (Adam might correspond to the lower bound, the last man who will die of cold to the opposite bound of comparison.) But the difference between 'father' and 'greater' shows itself for instance in that the former is not transitive (the father's father is not the father) while the latter is (if a is greater than b and b than c, then also a than c). Besides 'father' relates to animate things and 'earlier' to events.

(6) The difference between 'greater' and 'give' is not only that the former is two term and the latter three term; 'give' has no degrees (in the sense explained) and no 'bound'. Differences likewise exist between the corresponding substantives: 'giving' is a general name for actions, and 'magnitude' is the name of the system great–small.

(7) The advantage of working with formulae such as $x\ R\ y$ and the like is that it directs attention to what is logically essential. Symbolism represents the common intersection of rules so that other connections can be more readily ignored. However, with each formula we should consider whether it belongs to the grammar of our language or to that of some other spoken or constructed one; otherwise we confuse the meanings of signs in our language with constructed meanings.

(8) Relational sentences are to be distinguished from the fixing of a concept by means of a relation. If y is known then the relation 'x brother of y' can serve to fix x. It corresponds to the expression 'x is the one who beat y', when a report about the beating has already been given. These sentences define concepts and therefore can be neither true nor false.

For had x not beaten y, what is false is only the contained sentence 'x beat y', but not the definition. Only if *kinship* between x and y (their relation to each other) is to be expressed is 'x brother of y' a relational sentence.

13. PREDICATION (THE GRAMMAR OF THE COPULA)

(1) The copula 'is' has various functions. Often it is used in formulating definitions, for example 'the lion is an animal with such and such characteristics'. Here it marks a 'grammatical coordination'. (Coordination includes super- and subordination.) But the copula in '*this* grass *is* green' belongs to predication in applied language. The two differ in that the former belongs to what is laid down in language, while the latter presupposes such conventions and means: this object satisfies the conditions of the convention as to the use of 'grass' and 'green', here we have both grass and green.

(2) Consider three meanings of 'is': (i) definition, (ii) coordination, (iii) existence (for this last meaning, see the 'is' of existential sentences).

(3) The scholastics distinguish three kinds of supposition: (a) material, (b) logical and (c) real.

(a) 'Man is a monosyllabic word'. In this sentence something is asserted about the material used. It is a coordination in ordinary language and signifies that the material used to denote man in English has one syllable. One considers as it were the signs of a certain language or all languages and the various syllabic structures are ordered as to the number of syllables; in this way (by this sentence) the number of syllables 1 is coordinated with the sign 'man' (insofar as 'man' makes us think of its meaning as well, while with the syllables one thinks only of the material). The sentence so formulated does not belong to grammar.

(b) 'Man is a species'. Here we are talking about the concepts used and about their logical position. It is a typical sentence of grammar, because it treats of a concept's meaning and relations to the meanings of other concepts. One is not bringing man and animal into one system and species and genera into another in order to coordinate them, but it is part of the concept 'man' itself that it is a species, *so that the first array cannot be formed without the second.*

(c) 'The rose is beautiful'. Here we *apply* systems of language and therefore the sentence contains an assertion. That is what is meant by saying that it is an assertion about *reality*. For us, (a) and (c) are not different (unless (a) were a prescription for choosing the material). In both cases we have coordinations; but the 'is' in (b) marks a definition.

(4) Distinguishing the three suppositions is interesting in that we here discriminate between what has been laid down or observed in grammar and assertions (more precisely: all other kinds of sentence) in applied language. Besides we have here the important distinction between material and meaning (See Part One, III, 1).

14. HINTS FOR ANALYSING SENTENCES
(Characterization of the signs used in sentences.)

The task of analysing sentences is manifold. First comes the observation of the parts of speech to which the concepts in question belong; next, an indication of the special position of the concept in the given sentence (for through grammatical connections a word can acquire a meaning different from its ordinary one); then, the observation of the type of the sentence; and finally (if the sentence stands within a combination of sentences), the connection in which it appears, for example novel, history, physics and so on. On this see Part Two, IV, 7. (In Part Two, IV, we shall meet another kind of analysis where a combination is dismantled into single sentences.)

(1)   I II III
            John is coming

I = proper name of a person, follows the rules for proper names; invariant to spatio-temporal displacement. It can be observed by various senses (cross-section), and has a history whose gaps are filled by surmise and so on.

II. Predicative copula, goes with the verbal adjective (participle).

III. Activity of walking (or approaching in a vehicle) towards a goal (the goal may be merely imagined by the speaker); intransitive, present and so on. II and III together constitute a finite verb, transforming the activity into a state.

The whole is a statement that can be verified by sight, hearing, the statements of others (always presupposing knowledge of the concepts and their modes of application, and of the various conventions, for example that x's name is John).

(2)   I   II III   IV   V
            John is an important musician.

I. As in 1.

II. Marks a predicative sentence (the same as is contained in 'the important musician John...', or in 'John, the (an) important musician ...'. If the proper names of persons are set down on one side and their classes in order of skills on the other, then John belongs to the class of musicians).

III. Marks membership of a class (here the general name V). Number: singular (superfluous, because contained already in I). Ambiguous as to sex (not so in strongly inflected languages).

IV. Narrowing down of the general name, belongs to a two term system important–unimportant (but the criterion for the difference is vague).

V. A general name denoting a certain skill and training; a person (often metaphorically an animal but not inanimate objects), vague (but more precise than IV).

The whole statement is a coordination of the form $x \, \varepsilon \, \alpha$ where x is a proper name, α a class (general name). To verify such sentences, translate into 'In my judgement, ...' or 'if one asks people about John as a musician, they say that he belongs...' and the like.

(3)   I II   III   IV
            I see   a   house.

I. follows the rules for I (see personal pronouns).

II. Sense perception word of a simple sense object, transitive (pseudo-transitive); verb but not activity.

III. Indefinite article (marks membership of a general name one member being selected, though any other might take its place). Number: singular.

IV. General name, cross-section (perceivable by several senses).

The whole is a statement of sense perception relating to a cross-section.

The sign 'see' is used also to determine distance (observing whether something is nearer or farther) and to surmise whether the object belongs to this or that general kind; even concepts formed with the help of goals and values are 'seen'. That all this counts as seeing is a peculiarity of our language. The assessment of sense data and their combination with other systems is sometimes 'ascribed' to the sense of touch. In a dark room one says 'I am touching a glass'; as with seeing, *one* system is taken as point of departure. The missing systems are filled in by surmise and the whole is then called 'seeing' or 'touching' (with an index). Seeing or touching in such a sentence comprises reflections of various kinds. It is a different 'seeing' from 'seeing red', a different 'touching' from 'touching something hard'.

(4)   I   II   III   IV   V   VI   VII   VIII
        Anyone who cannot steer should not drive either.

I. Indefinite personal pronoun, indicates membership of a general name of human beings. (The general name is I to IV.)

II. Relative pronoun for persons, introduces the description of the general name.

III. An acquired disposition, with negation.

IV. A trained activity.

V. 'Key': normative sign.

VI. Negation.

VII. Activity as in IV.

VIII. Relates to what is common to the general name and the whole sentence, namely negation.

I to IV is not a subsidiary or prior clause but a concept, a general name denoting the lack of a certain disposition. The sentence is marked by 'should' (normative sign). It belongs to the group of universal advice or commands, depending on circumstances (the subsequent key).

(5)   A rider who has *one* horse should not take oats for two.

(Analyse this sentence in the same way!)

The phrase 'who has one horse' is not a subsidiary or parenthetic clause but a restriction on the extension of the general name 'rider'. If a similar sentence occurs in a *story*, for example 'a rider who had only one horse did not take oats for two', analysis would show the second part as a separate sentence, thus: (i) 'One of the riders had only one horse' and (ii) 'He took...'; but not in the mandatory sentence, where it is only *one* sentence.

(6)   I   II III IV   V   VI   VII   VIII
          Here one can call eternally before anyone hears.

I. Member of a vague, shiftable local system (a point of the here–there system).

II. and VII. 'indefinite' signs relating to people, no matter who.

III. Sign of disposition here to be translated into 'it is possible, probable, that...' or ' I have already... for a long time...'.

IV. Activity with an index showing purpose, aimed at a living creature.

V. Vague time indication, with exaggeration; to be translated into 'for a very (rather) long time'.

VI. Equivalent to 'previously' belongs to the three term system before–after–simultaneously. (Used for comparing events but here presumably in the expectation that the second event will never occur. Since the possibility of hearing is not excluded but envisaged, 'before' is here to be taken in the sense of 'before the time *when* someone hears'.)

VII. Anyone except the speaker in each case.

VIII. A perception word.

The whole sentence is an assertion or surmise.

(7)   I   II III   IV
          This rose is   beautiful.

I. Member of the two term ostensive system this–that, here used to transform a general name into a proper name having a history.

II. General name, plant.

III. Marks a type of sentence, namely predication which here contains also the time index of the present.

IV. Term of the two term system beautiful–ugly, summarizing experiences.

The whole sentence is an assertion, predication and singular proposition, verifiable by various people.

(These examples are meant only as general pointers to the manner of such analyses, which is thus contrasted with the currently usual subject–predicate analysis.)

CHAPTER IV

COMBINATIONS OF SENTENCES

1. Combinations of various kinds

(1) The expression 'combination of sentences' will be used in several senses, (i) for conjunctions of sentences by means of words that conjoin them like 'and', 'or', 'but', 'nevertheless' and so on (see 2). The most important mark that gathers them into a group is that their truth or falsehood entirely depends on the truth values of the constituents ('truth value' is short for 'truth or falshood'). This marks them off from (ii) combinations, whose truth values are independent of the truth values of the constituents (see Part Two, III, 3). (iii) To denote 'inferences' (see 4). (iv) To denote sentences that have a common key, for example history, physics, novel, fairytale, anecdote, song, prayer, grammar and so on. To this group belong the words (more correctly: fragmentary sentences) on title pages of books, such as 'Book of Fairy Tales', 'Text-book of Physics', 'English Grammar' and so on. They are indices relating to the grammatical location of the set of sentences in question. Such keys are met in single words, in certain word endings and in sentences; just as there are marks for question or exclamation, so too for combinations of sentences (see 7).

2. Logical particles

(1) We begin with some remarks on formality as such, applicable to the whole of logistic symbolism (which will however not be discussed in detail here).

(2) The word 'formal' is legitimately used in the sense of grammatical explanations as such (see Part One, II) or in the sense of a *one-sided* grammatical explanation that considers only part of the meaning (see Part Two III, 12). The word 'formal' is used also in another sense to denote linguistic *reforms*: one disregards the meaning of certain words in ordinary language and puts in their place a constructed meaning, as happens in some parts of mathematical logic. (This contributes to

confusion if not explicitly stressed.) A logical symbolism is to render the facts of language with a certain neatness, but not at the cost of *correct* representation.

(3) In saying that grammar is not concerned with reforms of language, one must be aware that 'correcting' certain expressions on the basis of rules that can be read off from language (correcting in the name of usage) does *not* fall under this head. The important difference between reform and 'correction' on the basis of existing and manifest rules is made clear by the following example: a book published in the 18th century is to be re-issued. Corrections can be made in two ways (i) the old spelling of regular participles ending in -t is changed into the present day -ed, which corresponds to *reform*. (ii) Printing mistakes in the sense of spellings not acceptable at the time of publication are changed to something then acceptable even if this deviates from present day spelling. This corresponds to *correction*. (It could then happen that a word that was accidentally spelled as it would be today is changed back into an old form.)

(4) One might ask: since any logistic sign, such as '*x*' (for word variables), '*R*' and '*f*' (function, property) has to be explained by means of ordinary language, why bother with symbolism? If somewhere one finds the sign '*x*', and one considers whether the word 'chair' or 'good' can be an '*x*', one must in any case consult actual usage to decide. Why, then, the detour? The answer is: for clarity. An engineer makes a schematic sketch of a machine, numbering each line and point; to each number the legend assigns a name that indicates what is meant, the meaning. This representation has the advantage of giving us a clear picture and helping us to eliminate unessential details. Just so, logical symbolism is more perspicuous. The symbols must be explained just as the lines and points of the sketch, for without explanation they have no meaning. But they are useful as aids, so long as they do not become alien to the structure of the language. (Those who lack all knowledge of symbolic logic can proceed to 5).

The conjunctions 'both–and' (p &q) and 'neither–nor' (p !q).

(1) 'And' mainly links sentences. The single conjoints are often fragmentary, which misleads one into regarding conjunction as a link between concepts; for example '*X* and *Y* and *Z* are going', which should really be analyzed into '*X* is going and *Y* is going and *Z* is going'.

(2) But conjunction can relate also to concepts. This happens in many 'grammatical sentences', where conjunction unites characteristics (points of different systems); as well as in other sentences: '*X* is between *Y and Z*', 'You, I *and* John are three people', 'two *and* two are four'. In a shop window one might read '*X* and *Y* cost ten pence' where the price is to be taken as meaning that *X* is sold only with *Y*. This sentence is thus not analysable into the two sentences '*X* costs five pence' and '*Y* costs five pence'.

(3) The schema for conjunction

p	*q*	*p & q*
T	*T*	*T*
F	*T*	*F*
T	*F*	*F*
F	*F*	*F*

or *TFFF* for short, symbolizes the linguistic expression 'both–and'; it is true if both *p* and *q* are. Since this conjunction may link commands too, one can introduce a symbolism in which *T*, *F* are replaced by *O*, *Ō* (obeyed and not obeyed). 'John is to fetch the axe and Jack is to carry the logs' (in the required sense of 'and') could be represented as

p	*q*	*p & q*
O	*O*	*O*
Ō	*O*	*Ō*
O	*Ō*	*Ō*
Ō	*Ō*	*Ō*

Such a calculus would help to combat the narrow view that logic deals only with assertions.

(4) Conjunction sometimes appears in the form of two signs (that is, each sentence carries a special sign); the two signs together constitute conjunction, for example 'both–and'. But sometimes it appears as *one* sign, such as 'and', 'but' and so on.

(5) The combination 'neither–nor' (*p!q*) is to be taken as true (obeyed) when neither *p* nor *q* are true (obeyed). The schema is

p	*q*	*p!q*
T	*T*	*F*
F	*T*	*F*
T	*F*	*F*
F	*F*	*T*

(6) For any logical particle, its truth schema is necessary but not sufficient. If someone says 'and' means *TFFF*' he points to a necessary characteristic, but he has given no sufficient indication of the place of conjunction in language, for conjunction is used only where there is some connection between the sentences conjoined (such as simultaneity of p and q; the same persons; identity of place and so on. This merely hints at the 'rule of connection', which needs to be further defined).

(7) 'And' and 'but': from the point of view of logic it was wrongly thought that 'but' was just a conjunction synonymous with 'and', as though the difference was one of *mere* psychological stress. However, not so: 'and' and 'but' do have common features as shown in their common truth schema, but in other respects they are *logically* different: 'John is going home *and* Bill is going home' is correct, 'John is going home *but* Bill is going home' is incorrect. Thus there is a difference.

(8) 'When John is tired he goes home $(=p)$ but when Bill is not tired he does not go home $(=q)$'. This combination is barred. For the word 'but' here relates to the contrast between the two men's behaviour and not to that between their states (tired and not tired). Since we can put 'John' in q and 'Bill' in p (as is indeed required by the rule of implication the rule of 'when' in the sense of 'only when', see below), this combination involves a misuse of the sign 'but' which here obviously relates to a *definite* contrast.

(9) 'But' contains 'and', but not conversely; for 'but' has the same truth schema and the 'rule of connection'. As to the additional rule of opposition, this can manifest itself by means of word order, stress and so on. But since the contrast consists in opposing the sentences in such a way as to produce a grammatical judgement of the joint sentences only, analysis does not show a third sentence. 'You study but I do not'. The 'but' shows only that the speaker knows that not to study is in contrast with to study, and that replacing 'I' by 'you' produces a contradiction.

(10) The opposition usually consists in the fact that replacing a sign in q by the corresponding sign in p produces a contradiction. But this condition is fulfilled only for opposition in pairs belonging to the same grammatical systems. However, the opposition often relates to a tacit expectation and so on, so that the sentence must be further analyzed before the opposition is revealed. For example, 'X is clever but not good'.

(11) 'A and B and C are going, but D and E are not'. Here we have

five statements linked by conjunctions. Here the members before 'but' may be interchanged, and those after 'but', but not across the 'but'. For example, we must not interchange A with D or E, for that would produce 'A is not going and B and C are going, but D is going and E not'. The sentences before 'but' and those after 'but' can be compared with brackets in arithmetic: $(a+b+c)-(d+e)$. (The grammar of the word 'but' as link between combinations of sentences will be dealt with elsewhere.)

(12) A semicolon often does the job of 'but', as a comma that of 'and'; in some cases several sentences are linked by commas except the last, which is preceded by 'and'. Rules about this (polysyndeton and asyndeton) belong to the grammar of the material since the comma or the dot of Russellian logic are just as suitable a material as the letters 'a-n-d'.

(13) The difference between 'and', 'but' on the one hand and 'partly–partly', 'now–now' on the other consists in that the latter contain marks that indicate the *kind* of belonging together of the sentences, whereas the two sentences may be contrasted, or joined by 'and', for *various* reasons. (That is why this combination can be regarded as a function and treated schematically.) But two sentences that somehow belong together, like 'I am going' and 'you are going' cannot be linked by 'partly–partly' and the like.

(14) Many conjunctions indicate that the two sentences are compatible: 'although...', 'even if..., nevertheless', 'however... still...' and so on. These are cases in which the events seem to occur in a certain order (or in a sequence similar to ground–consequence), but the expectation that the order exists is disappointed. To prepare someone for this fact one uses such phrases. These combinations contain the negation of a causal or ground–consequence sentence; such as: 'although released bodies fall to the ground, balloons rise', 'although b is left of a and c left of b, c is not left of a (in a circle)'.

(15) 'Firstly..., secondly..., thirdly...'. This conjunction contains linkage by 'and', just as applying ordinal numbers to sentences does. 'First..., then...' contains besides 'and' the two term system of succession. 'To begin..., next..., finally...' contains besides 'and' the fixing of a first and last point that are contrasted with the intervening points. 'Namely' and 'indeed' are not conjunctions nor is the colon; for they are subject to the rule that what comes after them is mostly a detailed explanation of what comes before (definition).

The Disjunctions p a q (p aut q) and p ∨ q (p vel q)

(1) The word 'or' in ordinary language usually occurs in the sense of 'either–or', corresponding to the Latin *aut*. For this combination the tule is that it is false when *p* and *q* have the same truth value, otherwise rrue. The schema is

p	q	$p\ a\ q$
T	T	F
F	T	T
T	F	T
F	F	F

or *FTTF* for short. This excludes the two cases 'both–and' 'neither–nor' (the first and fourth row of the truth values).

(2) However, we often meet an 'or' that might be schematically represented as T/F (*TTF*). If *A* says to *B*: 'I am going or you are', he may wish to exclude 'both–and' as well as 'neither–nor'; but more usually he will have no desire to pronounce on the former. In that case the first truth value could be either *T* or *F*.

(3) Finally, the disjunction p ∨ q excludes only 'neither–nor', but not 'both–and'; its truth values thus are *TTTF*.

(4) Disjunction too in the first place links sentences. If it links two words, then it is to be translated into a combination of sentences. But often it needs to be turned into a conjunction of sentences, as for instance with 'something is to be called *a* if it has shape *x* and colour *y* or *z*'. The disjunction between the concepts *y* and *z* is here to be transformed into a conjunction of sentences 'something is to be called *a* if it has shape *x* and colour *y and* something is to be called *a* if it has shape *x* and colour *z*'. (The 'and' link should not be translated; if it were, *other* sentences result: 'something is to be called *a* if it has shape *x and* something is to be called *a* if it has colour *y* or *z*'.)

(5) Disjunction may have several members: *paqaras*; just as conjunction has: *p & q & r & s*.

(6) We call *negation* of a combination of sentences the combination that is false if the former is true and conversely. On the other hand, we shall say that one combination excludes the other if the two differ in a *single* truth value: thus *p* and *q* excludes *p a q* (compare the truth schemata)

and conversely; but the negation of the disjunction $p \, a \, q$ is the combination that differs in each truth value, that is *TFFT*, which in words requires three links: "either 'both–and' or 'neither–nor'". In symbolic logic it is called equivalence and denoted by $p \equiv q$ and can be defined as the negation of exclusive disjunction:

The Implications: 'if–then' $(p \rightarrow q)$: 'only if–then': 'p materially implies q' $(p \supset q)$

(1) The combination of 'if–then' with negation yields the following four well-known modes: (i) if p, then q; p, therefore q. (ii) if p, then not-q; p, therefore not-q. (iii) if not-p, then q; not-p, therefore q. (iv) if not-p, then not-q; not-p, therefore not-q. These modes elucidate the link 'if–then' (modus ponens and modus tollens), they belong to the grammar of these words. The same is achieved by their truth schema:

p	q	$p \rightarrow q$	$p \rightarrow \bar{q}$	$\bar{p} \rightarrow q$	$\bar{p} \rightarrow \bar{q}$
T	T	T	F	–	–
F	T	–	–	T	F
T	F	F	T	–	–
F	F	–	–	F	T

where '$\bar{p}$' means 'not-p'.

The truth table is preferable to the other representation because it is 'richer', it displays more possibilities more vividly, as is obvious from comparing the two methods. The dash in the columns means that neither T nor F results in those cases, nothing has emerged. For we must distinguish this relation from that denoted by 'only if–then' which extends to cases of p being false. (The rules for 'if–then' will be described in detail elsewhere.)

(2) Insofar as the implication 'if–then' expresses what is common to the cause–effect and ground–consequence combinations of Chapter III, it is to be described as *formal*. (We may think of the symbol 'R' which stands for kinship relations and activities.) What is common (the intersection of the rules) is precisely what is represented in the truth schema. The textbook rules for the four modes must therefore be corrected in this sense. For example instead of stating the rule for the first mode $(p \rightarrow q)$ as 'with true ground, true consequence' we should say 'with true 'if'-sentence, true 'then'-sentence'.

(3) Implication is transitive: from $(p \to q)$ and $(q \to r)$ it follows that $(p \to r)$.

(4) The 'if-then' combination differs from the 'because' combination (because p, q) in that the truth values for the former are $T\ T/F\ F\ T/F$, while those for the latter are the same as for conjunction: the 'because' combination presupposes that both component sentences are true (it is false if either or both components are false).

(5) If $p \to q$ and p is false, q may be true or false: $T(T/F)\ F(T/F)$. But if $p \to q$ means 'only if p, then q', then we have the schema

p	q	$p \to q$
T	T	T
F	T	F
T	F	F
F	F	T

and similarly for $p \to \bar{q}$ and so on. This schema elucidates 'only if-then'.

In language, the combination of sentences 'only if-then' is often expressed in such a way that the form misleads one into wanting to put it as $(p \to q)\ \&\ (\bar{p} \to \bar{q})$. For example, 'if the weather is fine, I shall go for a walk and if the weather is not fine I shall not go for a walk'. But note that 'and' is here not a link between $(p \to q)$ and $(\bar{p} \to \bar{q})$, but an *addendum* to the 'if-then'. The combination of combinations $(p \to q)\ \&\ (\bar{p} \to \bar{q})$ is inadmissible, for there is a rule that a combination of combinations is barred if it has not at least one T and one F amongst its truth values.

(6) A says to B 'when I call out, you are to fix the rope to the cliff'. If A has not called but B nevertheless has fixed the rope, this cannot be regarded as obeying the command. If A has not called and B has not fixed the rope, one cannot say that B has not obeyed the command, but we are free to decide whether this is to count as obeying. For there is no uniform linguistic intersection for such cases. Therefore we shall represent the situation thus:

p	q	$p \to q$
T	O	O
F	O	$-$
T	$\bar{O}$	$\bar{O}$
F	$\bar{O}$	$-$

Since the if-sentence belongs amongst assertions while the then-sentence is an order, both $T-F$ and $O-\bar{O}$ are used. But if we put 'only if' instead of 'if', then the schema becomes $O\bar{O}\bar{O}O$.

(7) The double implication 'if p, then q and if q, then p', that is $(p \rightarrow q)$ & $(q \rightarrow p)$, has the truth values $T\ F\ F\ (T/F)$.

(8) The truth values of Russell's material implication $(p \supset q)$ are $T\ T\ F\ T$. One can imagine that there may be motives for introducing it, but it is different from the 'if–then' of language.

(9) Implications are combinations of sentences. They are subject to the rule that the sentences linked must stand in some sort of relation (ground–consequence or cause–effect). The implication 'if I climb Everest then this paper is white' is barred so long as no new convention has been laid down as to relation.

On New Formations and Reductions of Sentence Combinations

(1) A combination can be reduced to other combinations. This kind of reduction is especially interesting because it shows us how language is *formed* and what are the possibilities.

(2) There is no motive for introducing a special word for the combination 'I am walking or I am not walking' ($p\ a\ \bar{p}$). (Here we cannot have the combination $\vee$, because of the rule of contradiction. 'Or' must be meant in the sense of 'aut'.) For such a combination would always be 'true' (a tautology) and could not be used to convey information, commands and so on.

(3) But language does replace 'you and I' or 'Jack and Jill' by the word 'both'; 'Jack and Jill went but not Jack *or* Jill went' by 'both–and ...'; 'Jack did not go and Jill did not go' by 'neither–nor...'.

(4) Thus when we introduce similar abbreviations, reductions and transformation rules in symbolism, we are in the field of language formation.

(5) Such formations include $p \vee q$, $p \supset q$ insofar as they are not construed as *the* 'or' and *the* 'if' of common language; they do indeed conform with 'both–and', 'either–or', and so on, but they are new insofar as such combinations do not exist in a given language.

(6) The fact that such combinations have not been introduced goes back to a *lack of relevant motive* in practical life.

(7) However, one can *create* signs for obvious combinations; for

example p/q (the negation of conjunction) $=_{df} \overline{(p \ \& \ q)}$, that is 'not both p and q' or 'either not p or not q or neither p nor q', the sign for incompatibility' of p and q, introduced by Sheffer.

If combination operators are turned into substantives, then sentences that contain them are sentences of 'grammar'. Examples of such substantives are the concepts 'negation', 'conjunction', 'implication' and so on (the 'and', the 'or' and so on).

3. Tautology, rule, and analytic sentence

(1) Some rules of grammar are often confused with analogous tautologies. Tautologies are uninformative *combinations* of sentences occurring in applied language. A component sentence of a tautology can convey something (or express a command or desire); only on *combination* do the parts lose their function. A rule of grammar relating to combination of sentences differs from the corresponding tautology in that the rule as earlier explained, resembles a command, while the tautology is an empty assertion.

(2) The inference rule 'if p, then q; p, therefore q', according to Russell, differs from the tautology $[(p \supset q) \cdot p] \supset q$. But we must notice that $(p \vee q)$ $\supset (q \vee p)$ and the other tautologies can equally be taken either as tautologies or as rules, depending on the point of view. Suppose someone fixes the concept 'or' by introducing the rule that 'I am going or you are going' is to mean the same as 'you are going or I am going'; then $(p \vee q)$ $\supset (q \vee p)$ is a rule, or 'command' as to the use of signs (the formula has the advantage of not being earthbound, since any sentences can be put for p and q). But if someone uses such a combination within (applied) language after the concepts have been laid down (and not to exhibit their meaning), we speak of a tautology or a tautological combination of sentences.

(3) A tautology differs from an analytic sentence in that the latter is empty by virtue of the syntax of the isolated sentence alone, whereas a tautology is a combination whose trivial character is revealed only by the syntax of *combination*. The combination 'I am going or I am not going' is a tautology; the sentence 'this red body is coloured' is analytic. However, both may figure in grammatical observations (in our example, in order to elucidate the words 'or', 'coloured', 'red'). Analytic sentences and tautologies are sometimes called a priori.

(4) A sentence cannot at the same time be 'analytic' and 'synthetic', nor rule and statement. Only the *material* of the sentence can at times be the same.

(5) It is often said that logic consists of tautologies. Against this let us state explicitly that the sentences (rules) of logic are commands of a certain kind or grammatical observations (see earlier chapters) depending on the point of view. *But no rule of logic is a tautology,* for a command consisting of a tautological combination of sentences does not command anything, nor does a grammatical observation so made up state anything.

4. EXAMPLES OF DEDUCTION.
(THEORY OF INFERENCE)

(1) Inference is a combination of sentences in which the 'consequence' is derived from one or more 'premisses'.

(2) The traditional forms of inference belong to the grammar of the words 'all (every)', 'some (one)', 'none (not)'. They represent a combination of the systems all–some and affirmation–denial (whence *a, i, e* and *o* judgements).

(3) The word 'all' can be a mere abbreviation in cases where complete enumeration would be possible, for example 'all the days of the week', 'all the letters of the alphabet'. But it can be an independent concept where an enumeration is logically impossible, for example 'all men', 'all trees' and the like (for here enumeration cannot be uttered completely. The convention as to these concepts excludes enumeration. This 'all' may be replaced by partial enumeration and 'and so on', as in 'John, Jack and so on were present'. The two names are here meant as paradigms for the others: those who are not named must resemble those who are).

(4) To grasp the difference between the two meanings of 'all' let us recall the difference between proper and general names. 'Such and such a tree at such and such a time' is a proper name without 'history' (a 'snapshot'); 'such and such a tree' without the time indication is a proper name in the ordinary sense (See II, 1). But if in considering all trees *as such* one uses the word 'tree', one has gone over to a general name. Likewise for the difference between the two meanings of the concept 'all'.

(5) Moreover, 'all' may be meant as excluding 'none' but not 'some', or as contrasting only with 'some' without excluding 'none', or as

excluding both 'none' and 'some'. Whether one can infer from 'all' to 'some' depends on how one defines these concepts, which determines the rules of inference in a logical calculus.

(6) Similarly for 'some': as member of the pair 'some–none' it excludes only 'none' (=not none), as member of the system 'all–some' it stands in oppostion to all, and as part of the three term system 'all–some–none' it excludes 'all' and 'none'.

(7) 'All–some–none' can indeed constitute a closed three term system, in which case certain forms of inference hold; but one can regard 'all' and 'any' as a two term system ('some' is to mean 'not all', and 'not some' ='all'), in which case different forms of inference hold. (Compare the forms of inference in traditional logic and in modern mathematical logic.)

(8) As to deduction, one must ensure that the combination of sentences is marked as *grammatical* and not confused with any other.

(9) It is a merit of modern symbolic logic that it can distinguish between 'all men are mortal' and 'Socrates is a man', which in traditional logic count as of the same form: the former is a general (asymmetric) predication, the latter a subsumption of a single element.

(10) The 'theory of inference' is above all the grammar of the system of operations 'all–some–none'. Likewise, the theory of relations is the grammar of relative words, and the calculus of propositions the grammar of the logical particles (that is, the grammar of sentences, or their combinations, formed with the help of those words; for our language consists of sentences). All are equally valid, none is the 'one true logic'.

(11) There are besides many linguistic systems that can be built up into systems of deduction. As example of a deductive combination of sentences, consider the locution 'let alone'. Suppose I am near a window and I see a passer-by carrying a load of about a stone of iron and he shows signs of being tired which I recognize from his behaviour, and someone who is also looking out asks me 'could he not easily carry four stone?' I need no further experiments to answer this question, indeed I can say no at once. This is based on two things (i) general knowledge as to the lawlike and orderly character of natural events, that the greater load tires more. (ii) the logical inference: given this lawlike connection, one can deduce that in the present case he will not easily carry four, six, eight stone. Note that in the first step 'p, let alone q', one must bring in the natural law; for all subsequent steps deduction alone is enough. (In

that respect the matter runs as in 'all men are mortal'.) The deduction might for instance begin with the following observations: p, let alone q, q let alone r, therefore p, let alone r; for the combination with 'let alone' is transitive. 'Let alone' is not applicable to one and the same sentence, it is irreflexive: 'p, let alone p' is barred. Moreover it is asymmetric, one cannot have 'p, let alone q and q let alone p'. The converse of 'let alone' is 'not only–but also', or 'not only not–not even'.

(12) Consider the words 'similar', 'equal', and 'different' as basis for deduction. Some logical clarification of these words is called for first.

(13 In mathematics 'similar' (like 'equal') is symmetrical and transitive. Where no metric has been introduced, the meaning of 'similar' is different: there it is indeed often symmetrical but not necessarily transitive. (There is even a sense of 'resemble' and 'equal' where these concepts are asymmetrical, namely in comparisons aimed at explaining, in examples and the like. This meaning will here be ignored.) Thus a house A may resemble a house B and B resemble C without A having to resemble C. This holds wherever there is no 'metric', even when the system of comparison is stated, for example as to size. Two seen intervals may be equal, that is $A = B$, and $B = C$ (the two members of each separate pair are equal); but A might not equal C.

(14) With 'different from' it is different: once a metric is introduced and we have observed that a distance A is different from a distance B and B from C, it does not follow that A is different from C. Likewise if there is no metric: one might find for example that two shades of red, A and B, differ as do B and C, yet not A and C.

(15) 'Similar' is used in different senses (i) to express similarity of appearance. Thus two triangles that are geometrically similar or equal are often not so as to visual impression (if they stand at an angle or in other ways). (ii) geometrical similarity (as to measure and proportion). (iii) coincidence in many respects: book A resembles book B as to aim, form of sentences, size of chapters and so on.

(16) If in this last sense two things are so similar that in respect to the relevant systems in each case (in our way of putting it: for the requirements of living) they show no differences, then everyday language calls them 'equal', even if one could mention further systems to distinguish them (for example the way they were made, microscopic structure and so on).

(17) In such cases 'equal' is the limit of similarity, whence one cannot say 'more, most equal'. From this 'equal' we must distinguish combined forms like 'equally big', 'equally beautiful', for these signify 'equal' in respect of the given system. 'Equal' as such means: things coincide in so many relevant systems (in so many defining characteristics) that they 'resemble to the point of being indistinguishable'.

(18) 'Equal' can be meant as the opposite either of 'similar' or of 'different from'. As in so many cases, it depends on the members of the whole system. Notice these oppositions in the system 'similar–equal–different': 'similar–equal', 'similar-different', 'equal–different'. The concept 'equal' can be defined in such a way that it contains 'similar', so that with 'X is equal to Y' we should have also 'X is similar to Y'. 'Different' is to exclude both. As to symmetry and transitivity one has to lay down a convention. Thus one can build up a deductive system, a calculus, whose basic concepts are precisely these three words.

(19) Wherever subsumption and negation belong to the constitution of a system ('equal' contains 'similar' and means 'not different'), the formation of sentences by means of these words leads to a great many derived sentences.

5. SIMPLE AND COMPLEX SENTENCES

(1) The criterion for distinguishing simple from complex sentences is whether we can analyse it into several sentences, in order to understand, verify or obey it. If someone says 'this field is fertile', the sentence is complex insofar as one needs to understand or verify, both 'here is a field' and 'the field is fertile' to understand or verify the whole. (So long as the first remains unverified, one cannot tackle the second.)

(2) If in a letter someone writes 'I am telling you that the weather here is fine', the sentence is to be analyzed into 'the weather is fine here' and 'I am telling you this'; but the second is superfluous and empty, because it is merely an index to the first: if it were not a mark but an assertion, it would remain true even if the weather was not fine there. All marks such as 'I know that...', 'I surmise that...' do not lead us to describe a sentence as complex.

(3) All combinations that are mentioned in the 'vocabulary' likewise do not lead us to call a sentence complex. For example, 'here is a table'

can be analyzed into 'I see coloured surfaces here, arranged in a certain way and I have such and such tactile sensations (or used to have them when having similar visual sensations and simultaneously touching), and when others see similar things they usually say 'table', and... and...' (Such speech analyses are used only where one wishes to forestall misleading views, dismembering the original sentence into a series of others.) But since the word 'table' as word (as 'cross-section') already contains all this, we here speak of a *simple sentence*.

(4) The difference between simple and complex sentences relates to a given language. If ours lacked sentences like 'I am walking', 'he is walking', then 'we are walking' would be a simple sentence.

6. HINTS FOR ANALYSING CONNECTED SENTENCES

(1) Since the analysis of sentences in ordinary textbooks on grammar proceed uncritically and without reflection, it will be useful to call attention to the method of *critical* analysis by giving a few examples. Some hints must suffice since the topic is intended to become the object of a separate study. The syntax of conventional grammar (and the grammar of combinations of sentences) requires an even greater measure of criticism than morphology. Some examples will be taken at random from a textbook to contrast critical with traditional analysis. (Since we mean to criticize not a particular book but conventional grammatical analysis as such, we need not mention names. Any other textbook will provide similar examples for criticism.)

(2) The proper analysis of connected sentences does not change if we merely rearrange the parts without altering them, that is if no part is lost or rendered irrelevant or false or replaced by another part and the like. Conventional analysis changes with every rearrangement of the parts: this should lead us to reflect on the nature of analysis.

(3) Consider these examples: '*A* believes that one can be cured from any disease provided one perspires liberally before it is too late'. Conventional analysis produces this picture: main clause, subordinate clauses of first, second and third order. (Each step corresponds to a component sentence, or more correctly a group of words up to the next conjunctive expression.) Correct analysis: *A* believes the following universal causal conditional: 'if–then', which in individual cases yields

singular conditionals: 'if John breaks his arm and he perspires liberally, then...', 'if Jack catches a cold and..., then...' and so on. Of these derived sentences some may indeed be true, as for example the last mentioned. There is here no hierarchy of main and subordinate clauses as is given in traditional grammar: 'A believes' is not a sentence at all. (Could one verify it independently? Does it even make sense?) There is thus no reason for appointing these two words to the status of main clause. 'A believes' is the *key* of the sentence, which, depending on the meaning of 'believe', marks it (*A*'s sentence!) as subjunctive (believe = suppose) of indicative (believe = be convinced).

If-sentence and then-sentence are both 'main' sentences and hang inseparably together forming a conditional. The words 'before it is too late' are like 'liberally' a single indication (except that the former consists of several words).

(4) Ignoring this kind of example, what is supposed to be the meaning of main and subordinate sentence? Two procedures may be followed: (i) Main sentences are to be those sentences that can be recognized without 'translation' as assertions (or commands and so on). Subordinate sentences, in contrast, appear to start with as determinations of concepts, as indications of place or time (or other systems), which after analysis (translation) reveal themselves as asserted (or commanded) along with the rest. (ii) The part that carries the accent, the part that the speaker stresses and would be unwilling to give up, is to be called the main sentence. All other parts, even if they occur *explicitly* in the connected sentence, are to be subordinate. This may be different from case to case. But one might adopt an average corresponding to usage. Note that both methods admit connected sentences with *many* main sentences.

(5) With either method regard for the difference is grammatically interesting insofar as (i) teaches us to distinguish an explicit sentence from a 'contained' one, and (ii) leads us to the accent that controls verification. We recall what was said about stress in Chapter I, 12: in 'I am going to London on Wednesday' with the stress on London, the convention is that the sentence is false if I travel to Brighton instead; with the accent on 'going' and London deliberately neglected, the sentence often remains true even if I go to Brighton. Truth and falsehood depends on stress, which can underline a definite part as relevant or irrelevant. In this sense the main sentence is the part that is decisive for verification.

In this sense one can rearrange, making a main sentence subordinate and conversely. But if on complete rearrangement no parts appear any the less important (without loss of their truth within the connected sentence), then the sentence retains the same representation.

(6) 'I know how to build and mend a wireless set'. The usual analysis runs: main sentence, first subordinate clause (first order), second subordinate clause (first order). Notice again that 'I know' is not as such a sentence, but either an abbreviation or a mark of an indicative sentence, according to circumstance. Here the former applies: 'I can answer questions as to making or mending'. The negation of this sentence is the observation that one lacks these dispositions (though this lack does not yet amount to 'doubt' or 'query'; 'not to know' means that one cannot answer certain definite questions). Simple analysis produces 'I know how to build a set and I know how to mend one'. Each in turn is short for "If I am asked how one builds (mends) a set, then I answer: 'one builds (mends) a set by doing such and such', and this answer is correct".

(7) 'I could not discover where, when and how he (X) had travelled'. This sentence must first be analysed into 'I could not discover where he had travelled' and 'I... when...' and 'I... how...'. Each of these is then not to be dissected into two parts, 'I could not discover' and 'where (when, how) he had travelled'. For these parts are not sentences. Rather, the sentence must be analysed thus: 'X has travelled', 'I am trying to discover his destination and I have failed', and likewise for the parts with 'when' and 'how'. Notice that analysis could be pushed further. Thus 'X has travelled' could be dismantled into 'X made such and such movements' and so on. But this is irrelevant here. Similar analyses were discussed in Chapter III.

(8) 'When John left he said he would return at six'. Incorrect analysis: subordinate clause of first order, main sentence, subordinate clause of first order. But notice that 'when John left' is no more a sentence than 'at six'; both are time indications, except that 'at six' is usually more precise than 'when John left' (for the reference system of the first is universally known: the clock). But 'John left' is a sentence contained in this connected sentence. 'He said' without *what* he said is no sentence at all (unless one meant articulation of certain sounds which is evidently not the case here). 'John returns at six' is indeed a sentence but it is not contained in the original. If he failed to return at six, the sentence would

be false but the original to be analysed could nevertheless be true. Correct analysis might run thus: 'John left', "He said (on leaving): 'I shall return at six'". To call this a temporal sentence because of the 'when' is no more justified then calling 'I shall begin to write at three' a temporal sentence because it contains the sign 'three (o'clock)'.

(9) Attributive determinations are to be translated into independent sentences: 'the ripe fruits on the topmost branches of that old mulberry tree are black' becomes 'there stands a mulberry tree', 'it is old', 'it has branches', 'the branches are at various heights', 'the branches bear fruit', 'the fruit are ripe', 'the fruit are black'.

(10) Beware of a seemingly logical sham analysis! An example of one such is the resolution of a universal statement into a conjunction (without adding the 'and so on'). For example 'All men' = man A, man B and man C. Likewise 'a man' is not the same as man A or man B or man C. It is likewise incorrect to translate the question as to the cause of an event into a disjunctive question: 'Is A or B or C the cause of the event?' In this question the sign 'cause' is not a technical abbreviation for the single causes that we might enumerate, rather it relates to all events past or possible and therefore logically not enumerable. There are also questions as to the cause where a certain number of relevant events are being considered, but then the question means something else, being short for 'Is A, B or C the cause?'

(11) 'While X stayed inside at his birthday party Y went for a walk'. Analysis: (i) Y went for a walk. (ii) X stayed inside. (iii) His birthday party was being given there. (iv) The facts in (i) to (iii) were simultaneous. (Moreover, the sentence might invite us to be indignant, or wish to exclude the expectation that Y would be there if X and Y are friends.) To call (i) the main sentence seems arbitrary, as does giving a higher rank (first order) to (ii) than to (iii).

(12) 'When Hume, having left Italy, returned to England, where his *Enquiry* had meanwhile been published, he found that it had met with little more response than his earlier and difficult *Treatise*'. This connected sentence would traditionally be analyzed as follows: subordinate clause of first order (first part), subordinate clause of second order, subordinate clause of first order (second part), subordinate clause of second order, main sentence. Correct analysis: (i) Hume left Italy; (ii) Hume returned to England (after (i)); (iii) Hume had written the *Enquiry* (before (i));

(iv) This was published in England (after (iii) and before (i)); (v) Hume had written the *Treatise* (before (iii)); (vi) The *Treatise* had been published (before (iv)); (vii) The *Treatise* had little initial success; (viii) The *Enquiry* had not much more initial success; (ix) Hume recognizes (viii)); (x) The *Treatise* is difficult. Furthermore (xi) difficult books are badly received; (xii) because the *Treatise* is difficult, it was badly received. (xi) and (xii) are causal sentences, the former stating a general connection, the latter a particular instance. If one of these sentences were false most of the others could nevertheless be true. But (ii) presupposes (i), and (xii) presupposes (xi). If (ix), the 'main sentence', were false, the others could all be true. If (viii) were false, then so would (ix), but the rest could all be true.

(13) We leave the reader to take other examples and treat them similarly.

7. TYPES OF SENTENCE COMBINATIONS

(1) History, physics, novel, fairy tale, anecdote, prayer, song, myth, dream, grammar and so on, are designations relating to sentence combinations, pointing to their function in life, to their mode of verification and so on.

(2) Sentences within such a combination are universally assumed to be uniform with regard to it. This may be called the assumption for that combination: where it fails, sentences are isolated. A word belonging to a certain part of speech will be followed by others belonging to different parts of speech. A sentence of a certain type is followed by sentences of different types. All this occurs within *one* combination of sentences. But the change to a different type of combination must be marked explicitly. A full stop (or the capital letter at the start) marks merely the end (or beginning) of a single sentence or combination of sentences in the sense of 2 and 6; the 'assumption of the combination' remains independently of this.

(3) To make this clearer, consider the following situation: a bookbinder by mistake assembles leaves from different books, so that page 17 from a biography is followed by page 18 of a textbook of grammar, and page 20 of a novel by page 21 of a different novel. Suppose the last sentences on pages 17 and 20 finish with a full stop. The reader on perusing the first sentences on pages 18 and 21 would begin by misranging them. But on page 21 this would not produce a grammatical misunderstanding,

since the type of combination remains the same. Even if he did relate a word such as 'him' that might occur there to another person, namely the one that was being discussed on page 20, this is merely as though someone was speaking about John and the hearer relates it all to Jack. But in the first sentence on page 18 we have in *addition* a *grammatical misunderstanding*. For here the key of the combination has been mistaken, so that the sense of the sentence becomes different.

(4) In speech as in writing, if no change is indicated, if no new conversation is in evidence, everything is to be understood in the sense of what went before, on the assumption that the previous circumstances continue to hold. In this respect verbal communication resembles life in general, where we likewise presuppose the order that happens to prevail and assume the familiar course of events so long as we learn nothing to the contrary. If I read a letter and have reached the fourth sentence, I will not want suddenly to assert or suppose that the fifth was written by someone else (assuming I discover no changes in style and so on). Hence the convention for combinations, that the first sentence after a change should be marked with a special sign of transition.

(5) A sudden change of period, even of the year and day, must be marked even within a given combination; but that the first event reported *preceded* the second is taken for granted. This holds for combinations that report on events and so on, here called 'historical combinations of sentences': in these the convention is that the sequence of sentences pictures the sequence of events. Occasionally the chain is broken by simultaneities, references to the past and so on, but such points must be specially marked so as to preserve the presupposed 'flow of time'. Historical combinations contain only sentences about the past and causal sentences to be verified in future. By this and similar conventions it differs from the combination that may be called 'causal' or 'physical' (for example physics, biology, psychology and so on). The sentences of that combination do not relate to what occurred only at one given place and time, so that the above conventions do not apply.

(6) Historical combinations treat of events and so do the physical. What is the same and different for the two may be explained as follows: historical combinations often speak of many events, as do the physical. For example 'the army of Alexander the Great advanced'. This reports on an almost indescribably large sum of single events (for every movement

of every part of every man is an event). So the physical sentence 'all bodies expand when heated' reports on many events at once. But the difference is clearly noticeable: the historical sentence might equally well report on a single event, but the physical sentence could not. (This is a logical veto!) Historical sentences report only on past events, physical sentences on past and future at once. (Indeed, the main interest lies in their reference to the future.) The complex sentence of a historical combination can be analyzed into a *finite* number of sentences; but a physical sentence makes the claim that it holds at any place and time: the number of sentences to be derived from it cannot be finite. Time is important in both types. The regularity of events speaks of their course in time in the same way as the report on the single events that have occurred in time. But in the physical case regularity is not tied to a unique time span, whereas in a historical report we cannot put t_1 for t_2. ('Tomorrow it will rain' is about the future but relates to a unique event; this sentence thus partly resembles the historical and partly the physical. It is a 'singular forecast'. A combination consisting of such may be called 'prophecy'.)

(7) For many 'poetic combinations', such as the novel, the conventions as to temporal sequence and marking of big changes in time and changes of place do indeed hold; but in contrast to the previous two types, we here have the different convention that ordinary verification is to be avoided (that one is not to use the $T-F$ system in its ordinary sense). In novels one distinguishes three types of sentence (i) those in which proper names and indications of place and time are to be treated only as variables, so that other signs of the relevant parts of speech may be substituted. The only requirement is that the account should be *typical*. In this respect a novel may be compared with a landscape painting, where the point is that we do meet similar landscapes. In this sense the sentences of a novel resemble those of science. Sometimes we may even be concerned with fairly precise predictions about behaviour. If it were a historical combination one would have to say of many sentences that they were false (that is, they report on events that did not take place). The term 'poetic' signifies the convention that one refrains from this, so that a combination that is on the whole a typically correct description is said to contain much 'poetic truth'. (ii) in many sentences the names (and indications of place and time) are not completely variable. (The

name 'Christian' would not fit into Shakespear's 'Troilus and Cressida.'
Similarly for certain indications of space and time; thus 'anachronisms'
may occur: in the play mentioned, Hector of Troy quotes Aristotle!)
To that extent these are imprecise historical sentences that manifest
themselves in the choice of detail mentioned. To this class belong many
sentences that characterize a *definite* setting. On translation, they become:
'In Greece, at the time of... conditions were somewhat like those described'; "in that historical setting such and such behaviour was current'
and so on. Sentences of type (i) and (ii) require much difficult translation
before they can be verified (after 'removing brackets' from the combinations). (iii) Since the writer often imitates a historical combination,
there are some sentences that are not to be translated, but are inserted
merely to assimilate the story to an historical account. (Indications of
place and time in a novel are often genuine, required to describe a
certain setting: these are historical sentences; but they might also be
fictitious indications that are meant to simulate historical sentences for
the purpose of assimilation to an historical account.)

(8) 'Once upon a time...' is the key of fairy tales and signifies that
the sentences conveyed are not historical, nor do they represent typical
recurrent situations, but that the sequel will string together phantastic
imaginations gathered into a 'tale'. Hence indications of space and time
are irrelevant. 'Once upon a time' indeed almost means 'never'.

(9) Anecdote and joke are marked by the fact that they present
situations that tend to provoke a feeling of fun. Both contain sentences
that may be historically or physically verified, but such verification is
entirely omitted, because the operative convention declares it to be
irrelevant. Usually it is grammatical solecism or strange behaviour that
generates a sense of the ridiculous. (Tracking down the 'mistake' in
grammatico-logical jokes is one of the logically most interesting tasks.)
The joke as a whole may be 'good' or 'bad', but the individual sentences
are not answerable to such a system. They are outside the 'grammatical
dualisms' that mark individual types of sentence (that is, outside the
systems true–false, obeyed–not obeyed, fulfilled–not fulfilled, answered–
not answered).

(10) Requests and advice are commands of a certain kind: they cannot
be true or false, but accepted or rejected (followed or not followed).
A prayer is a request to God or other beings satisfying certain conditions:

(i) they understand our language (ii) they are more powerful than we are and can make our wishes come true (iii) they are occasionally influenced by our requests to fulfil our wishes. But other combinations that resemble these only in certain respects are often called 'prayer' too; to resolve conflicts, to struggle free from mental distress, a person often prays without expecting this to produce fulfilment of a wish. For the linguistic average, his sentences are prayers, but for him they are to be compared with music, song and so on. Music and lyrical poetry too can express ideas, and can be understood and translated. To that extent we are concerned with signs, sentences and language; but for the rest, music and poetry do not consist of signs or sentences. (Compare also 'mechanical' prayers, such as the Buddhist 'omani pad me um' and the like.)

(11) If a myth is put into the form of a historical sentence combination, this may make true sentences false. For although the new combination resembles the original one in that to each name or sentence of the one corresponds a name or sentence of the other ('similarity' in the geometrical sense), nevertheless the two keys differ and therefore the meanings of many signs are different in the two (see II, concepts of phantasy). Likewise the sense of individual sentences is different in the two combinations, since that depends on the meanings of the words and on the keys. Take for example a sentence from the myth: 'god X first lived on mountain Y but later went to valley Z'; as a mythical sentence this may be true for us, for on translation it reads 'the inhabitants of the particular region used to believe that...' (which may be further and more precisely analyzed). The designation 'myth' just means this translation. But if we transform the combination into an historical one, putting hero A in place of god X, the sentence may become false, if we learn that that hero lived neither on the mountain mentioned nor migrated to the valley. This is to show the difference between a mythical and an historical combination.

(12) The same can be done without change of key: if the actual history of a tribe is transformed into a history of the tribal ancestor, the sentences are falsified although the general key remains the same. For a sentence like 'the tribe went from X to Y' means 'every (or most of the) then living members went from X to Y', whereas the same sentence relating to the tribal ancestor reports on the journey of a single man.

(13) From the point of view of the waking state, *dreams* denote a

sentence combination whose sentences and concepts carry a certain index. One might think that dreams were a confused combination of concepts. But actually dreams contain very little more nonsense than the waking state. Sentences uttered in dreams, or thought in silence, are not of much use for finding one's bearing when awake, because they often represent events in quite a different order. It is easier to embed the dream sentences into the wakeful ones as 'dream memories' than the other way round. In logic, which recognizes all orders as equally valid and has no preferred sequence for events, this is not a mistake. That there sometimes are nonsensical word combinations is nothing peculiar to dreams. The difference is at best one of degree. If the whole world were a dream, as poets have it, if we always lived in a dream, if Descartes' demon gave us daily film shows, that would in no way impair our language. It would merely give a different description for the adventitious order of events in the world. The newly created conditions of life might indeed produce other grammatical forms, but all this happens equally in the waking state.

(14) In 'dream-memory' the concepts used in the dream undergo a change of meaning: to us 'water' means something accessible to the senses. If we see a picture of water on a screen or a photograph we call it water because it pictures real water. But that is accessible to touch, too. In a film show of a swimming contest, a man said to his son 'look, what a big stretch of water!' and the boy replied 'false water!' He wanted to point to the difference between the two meanings of 'water'. Looking at events on the cinema screen may be compared with dreaming. So long as we do not mark the combinations with the index 'dream' or 'film', the concepts have the same meaning as in the waking state and the sentences are to be verified in the same way that we usually adopt. Only when indices are attached do some words change their meaning. With cross-sections it is often the meaning that they have in discussions about photographs. But other kinds of words too change their 'location', and sentences likewise.

BIBLIOGRAPHICAL APPENDICES

A. *Works Used by the Author*

No books are directly referred to in these *Prolegomena* but the author records (in a letter of 3 September 1973) that the following are works that he studied more or less closely in the years up to 1935 and that have an indirect connection with the ideas of the *Prolegomena*.

[1] Brentano, F., *Psychologie vom empirischen Standpunkte*, Leipzig 1874. [Transl. by Linda L. McAlister *et al.*, *Psychology from an Empirical Standpoint*, London 1973].

[2] Carnap, R., *Der logische Aufbau der Welt*, Berlin 1928. [Transl. by R. A. George, *The Logical Structure of the World*, London 1967.]

[3] Couturat, L., *Die philosophischen Prinzipien der Mathematik*, German translation by G. Siegel, Leipzig 1908. [French original: *Les principes des mathématiques*, Paris 1905.]

[4] Frazer, J. G., *The Golden Bough*, London 1890 (1st edn.), 1900 (2nd edn.), 1911–20 (3rd edn.).

[5] Frege, G., *Die Grundlagen der Arithmetik*, Breslau 1884. [Transl. by J. L. Austin, *The Foundations of Arithmetic*, 2nd edn., Oxford 1953.]

[6] Hilbert, D. and Ackermann, W., *Grundzüge der theoretischen Logik*, Berlin 1928. [Transl. by L. M. Hammond *et al.*, *Principles of Mathematical Logic*, New York 1950.]

[7] Husserl, E., *Logische Untersuchungen*, Halle 1900. [Transl. by J. N. Findlay, *Logical Investigations*, London 1970.]

[8] Husserl, E., *Ideen zu einer reinen Phänomenologie und phänomenologischer Philosophie*, Halle 1913. [Transl. by W. R. B. Gibson, *Ideas, General Introduction to Pure Phenomenology*, London 1931.]

[9] Kant, I., *Kritik der reinen Vernunft*. [Various translations as *Critique of Pure Reason*, etc.]

[10] Mach, E., *Analyse der Empfindungen*, 4th edn., Jena 1918. [Transl. by

C. M. Williams and S. Waterlow, *The Analysis of Sensations*, Chicago 1914.]

[11] Reichenbach, H., *Philosophie der Raum-Zeit-Lehre*, Berlin 1928. [Transl. by M. Reichenbach and J. Freund, *The Philosophy of Space and Time*, New York 1958.]

[12] Russell, B., *Die Probleme der Philosophie*, German edition, Erlangen 1926. [English original: *Problems of Philosophy*, London 1912.]

[13] Russell, B., *Einführung in die mathematische Philosophie*, German edition, Munich 1923. [English original: *Introduction to Mathematical Philosophy*, London 1919.]

[14] Schlick, M., *Allgemeine Erkenntnislehre*, Berlin 1918 (2nd edn., 1925).

[15] Schlick, M., Erleben, Erkennen, Metaphysik, *Kantstudien*, Vol. 31 (1930).

[16] Schlick, M., Die Wende der Philosophie, *Erkenntnis*, Vol. 1, Leipzig 1930.

[17] Schmidt, W. and Koppers, W., *Völker und Kulturen*, Regensburg 1924.

[18] Whitehead, A. N. and Russell, B., *Principia Mathematica*, Cambridge 1910–1913.

[19] Wittgenstein, L., *Tractatus Logico-Philosophicus*, London 1922.

B. *Publications by the Author*

The following are Dr Schächter's main publications (as selected by himself) subsequent to 1935.

[1] *Mavo Kazar l' Logistikah* [in Hebrew; *A Short Introduction to Logistik*, Vienna, Viktoria-Verlag, 1937. With a Foreword by Prof. Hugo Bergmann].

[2] Bijdrage tot de analyse van het begrip 'cultuur' [Contributions to the Analysis of the Concept 'Culture'], *Synthese* Vol. 2 (1937) 47.

[3] Religie en wetenschap [Religion and Science], *Synthese* Vol. 2 (1937) 159.

[4] Over het wezen der philosophie [On the Nature of Philosophy], *Synthese* Vol. 2 (1938) 395.

164   PROLEGOMENA TO A CRITICAL GRAMMAR

[5] Der Sinn pessimistischer Sätze [The Sense of Pessimistic Proposi-
tions], *Synthese* Vol. 3 (1938) 223.

[6] *Syntaxis* [in Hebrew], Mizpeh Publishing Co., Tel-Aviv, Palestine
1944.

[7] Ueber das Verstehen [On Understanding], *Synthese* Vol. 8 (1949)
367.

[8] *Mi'Mada, L'Emunah* [in Hebrew; *From Understanding to Faith*].
Copyright 1953 by the Association of Hebrew Writers and the
Dvir Co., Tel-Aviv, Israel, 2nd edn., 1964.

[9] *Mavo L'Talmud* [in Hebrew; *An Introduction to the Talmud* (partly
from a logical point of view)], Dvir Co., Tel-Aviv, 1954. (Textbook,
13th edn. to date.)

[10] *Pirke Ha-Drakhah B'Tanakh* [in Hebrew; *Guide to the Old Testament*], Copyright by the publisher: M. Newman, Jerusalem/Tel-Aviv,
1960.

[11] *Shvilim B'Hinukh Ha-Dor* [in Hebrew; *Directions in Contemporary
Education*], Aleph-Verlag, Tel-Aviv, 1963.

[12] *Ha-Al Enushi B'Enushi* [in Hebrew; *Man and Human Excellence
(Logical and Ethical Essays)*], Aleph-Verlag, Tel-Aviv, 1963.

[13] *Otzar Ha-Talmud* [in Hebrew; *Talmudical Thesaurus,* (a lexicon of
its terms, fundamental concepts, and important rules)], Dvir Co.,
Tel-Aviv, 1963, 2nd edn.

[14] Jehezkel Kaufman: New Vistas in Bible Studies, *Ariel,* A Review
of the Arts and Sciences in Israel (Cultural Relations Department,
Ministry of Foreign Affairs, Israel), 1964.

[15] *Jahaduth W'Hinukh B'sman Hase* [in Hebrew; *Judaism and Education in Modern Times*], Dvir Co., Tel-Aviv, 1966.

[16] The Task of the Modern Intellectual, in *An Anthology of Hebrew
Essays,* Vol. II, pp. 299–310, Institute for the Translation of Hebrew
Literature and Massada Publishing Co., 1966.

[17] *Mavo L'Tanakh* [in Hebrew; *Introduction to the Old Testament* – A
new version of No. 10], Niv-Verlag, Tel-Aviv, 1968.

[18] *Pirke Ijun L'newukhe S'manenu* [in Hebrew; *Reflections on Dilem-
mas of our Time, Essays*], Dvir Co., Tel-Aviv, 1970.

[19] *B'Prosdor L'Hashkafath Olam* [in Hebrew; *Gate to a Philosophical
Creed, Essays*], M. Newman, Jerusalem/Tel-Aviv, 1972.

VIENNA CIRCLE COLLECTION